SCHOLASTIC

MW00605260

100 *Mini* Task Cards
Literary Text

Reproducible Mini-Passages With Key Questions to Boost Reading Comprehension Skills

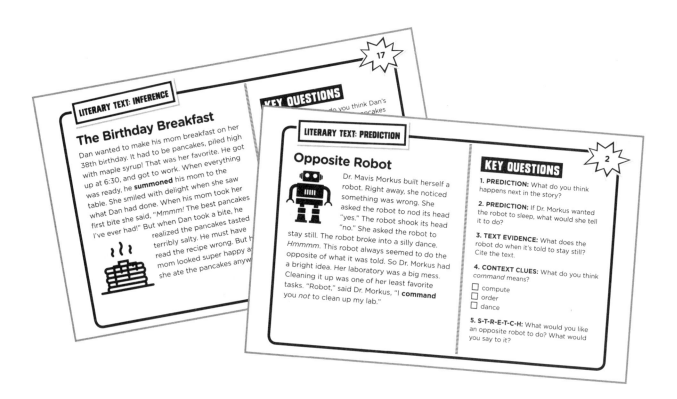

LITERARY TEXT: INFERENCE

The Birthday Breakfast

Dan wanted to make his mom breakfast on her 38th birthday. It had to be pancakes, piled high with maple syrup! That was her favorite. He got up at 6:30, and got to work. When everything was ready, he **summoned** his mom to the table. She smiled with delight when she saw what Dan had done. When his mom took her first bite she said, "*Mmmm!* The best pancakes I've ever had!" But when Dan took a bite, he realized the pancakes tasted terribly salty. He must have read the recipe wrong. But h... mom looked super happy a... she ate the pancakes anyw...

KEY QUESTIONS

17

...do you think Dan's ...pancakes

LITERARY TEXT: PREDICTION

Opposite Robot

Dr. Mavis Morkus built herself a robot. Right away, she noticed something was wrong. She asked the robot to nod its head "yes." The robot shook its head "no." She asked the robot to stay still. The robot broke into a silly dance. *Hmmmm.* This robot always seemed to do the opposite of what it was told. So Dr. Morkus had a bright idea. Her laboratory was a big mess. Cleaning it up was one of her least favorite tasks. "Robot," said Dr. Morkus, "I **command** you *not* to clean up my lab."

KEY QUESTIONS

2

1. PREDICTION: What do you think happens next in the story?

2. PREDICTION: If Dr. Morkus wanted the robot to sleep, what would she tell it to do?

3. TEXT EVIDENCE: What does the robot do when it's told to stay still? Cite the text.

4. CONTEXT CLUES: What do you think *command* means?

☐ compute
☐ order
☐ dance

5. S-T-R-E-T-C-H: What would you like an opposite robot to do? What would you say to it?

New York • Toronto • London • Auckland • Sydney
Mexico City • New Delhi • Hong Kong • Buenos Aires

Mini-passages written by Carol Ghiglieri and Justin Martin
Cover design by Tannaz Fassihi
Cover photo © Mieke Dalle/Getty Images
Interior design by Grafica, Inc.
Interior illustration by The Noun Project

ISBN: 978-1-338-11300-6

4 5 6 7 8 9 10   40   23 22 21 20 19 18

CONTENTS

INTRODUCTION

Welcome to *100 Task Cards: Literary Text!*

The human brain is hard-wired for stories; every culture on earth immerses its younger generation in tales that entertain and explain the complicated ways of the world. There's no doubt about it—kids need narratives! That said, many students are not achieving "deep comprehension" because they fail to master basic reading skills, including the ability to make inferences, assess a narrator's point of view, understand characters, visualize a setting, accrue new vocabulary words via context clues, or isolate a story's primary theme. And, with the rigorous literacy standards currently in place, that means children may be failing on standardized tests, too.

But don't despair. This practical resource is here to help your students vastly improve their comprehension skills—and meet your challenging state standards—in just minutes a day! The 100 literary task cards in this book offer motivating mini-passages with key questions related to:

- **Prediction**
- **Inference**
- **Character**
- **Setting**
- **Point of View**
- **Tone**
- **Theme**
- **Compare and Contrast**
- **Conflict and Resolution**
- **Cause and Effect**

The cards are designed for instant use—just photocopy, cut them apart, and they're good to go. They are also designed for flexible use. These riveting texts are perfect for seat work, centers, or meaningful homework. They're great for independent practice or work with partners, small groups, or even the whole class.

The questions on the cards, which can be responded to in writing or orally, will help students hone critical comprehension skills they'll rely on for a lifetime. And here's more good news: Because the mini-passages were written by professional authors with a gift for engaging young readers, kids will absolutely *love* them!

So what are you waiting for? Read on for tips that will help your students grow into confident, fluent, engaged readers—quickly and painlessly. And don't forget to look for the other great books in this series, including *100 Task Cards: Informational Text* and *100 Task Cards: Text Evidence.* The kids in your class will thank you.

TEACHING TIPS

About the 100 Literary Task Cards

This book contains 100 cards, each presenting a literary mini-passage. The stories vary by genre, form, purpose, and tone in an effort to give students a rich variety of reading material that correlates with current state standards. (For a list of those standards, see page 8.) Each card contains five key questions, including one related to context clues. This special feature is intended to boost your students' ability to glean the meaning of unfamiliar words they encounter in all texts.

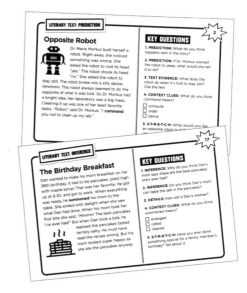

The cards address the following ten topics: prediction, inference, character, setting, point of view, tone, theme, compare and contrast, conflict and resolution, and cause and effect. You will find the target skill in the left-hand corner of each card. The mini-passages can be used in any order you choose. However, if you are teaching a certain topic or wish to help students master a particular skill—such as prediction—you can simply assign one or more cards from that category.

SAMPLE CARD: Here's a quick tour of a task card.

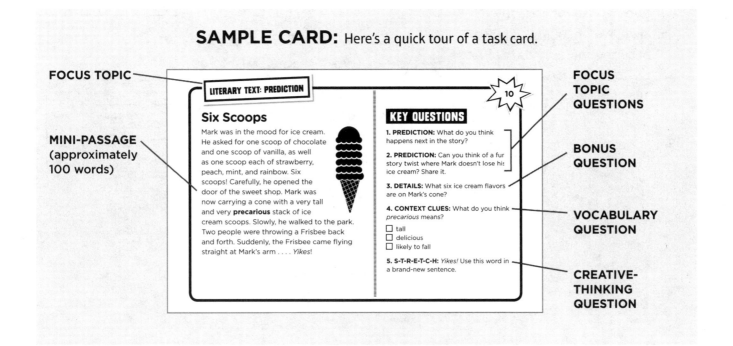

FOCUS TOPIC

MINI-PASSAGE (approximately 100 words)

FOCUS TOPIC QUESTIONS

BONUS QUESTION

VOCABULARY QUESTION

CREATIVE-THINKING QUESTION

About the 14 Comprehension Helper Cards

To scaffold student learning, we've provided 14 Comprehension Helper Cards. (See pages 9–15.) These "reference" cards—with topics ranging from inference to figurative language—are intended to provide age-perfect background information that will help students respond knowledgeably to the five questions on the cards. We suggest you photocopy a set for students to refer to as they work through the 100 task cards.

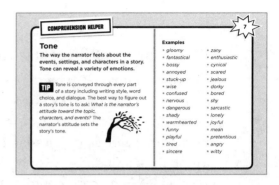

About the Answer Key

We've also included a complete answer key. (See pages 67–80.) In the key, we've provided sample responses to the questions on all 100 cards. Please note that some answers will vary. Because many of the questions are open-ended and no two minds work exactly alike, we encourage you to accept—and applaud—all reasonable answers.

MAKING THE TASK CARDS

The task cards are easy to make. Just photocopy the pages and cut along the dashed lines.

- **Tip #1:** For sturdier cards, photocopy the pages on card stock and/or laminate them.

- **Tip #2:** To make the cards extra appealing, use different colors of paper or card stock for each category of card.

- **Tip #3:** To store the cards, use a plastic lunch bag or a recipe box. Or, hole punch the corner of each card and place on a key ring.

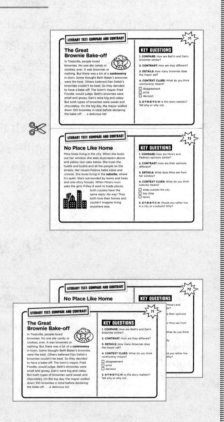

First-Time Teaching Routine

Any text will become accessible to students who bring strong reading strategies to the table. Here's an easy routine for introducing the task cards to your students for the very first time.

1. Display an enlarged version of the task card using an interactive whiteboard, document camera, or overhead projector.

2. Cover the mini-passage and display only the title. Read it aloud and invite students to predict what the story will be about.

3. Read the mini-passage aloud, slowly and clearly.

4. Boost fluency by inviting a student to read the mini-passage again using his or her best "performance" voice.

5. Discuss the mini-passage. Encourage students to comment and to connect it to other stories as well as their own lives.

6. Call attention to the five key questions to the right of the mini-passage.

7. Challenge students to respond thoughtfully to each question. **TIP:** Use a highlighter to mark clues to the answers within the text.

8. Number and record each answer on a chart pad. Model using complete sentences with proper spelling and punctuation.

9. Build comprehension by working with students to craft a brand-new question related to the text. Then, answer it.

10. Give your class a round of applause for successfully completing a task card. Now they're ready to tackle the cards independently.

INTEGRATING THE TASK CARDS INTO THE CLASSROOM

The task cards can be used in many ways. Here are ten quick ideas to maximize learning:

- Challenge students to complete one task card every morning.

- Invite partners to read the task cards together and respond in writing.

- Invite small groups to read, discuss, and respond to the task cards orally.

- Place the task cards in a learning center for students to enjoy independently.

- Carve out time to do a task card with the whole class a few times a week.

- Encourage individual students to build fluency by reading a task card aloud to the class. They can then solicit from fellow students answers to the questions.

- Laminate the task cards and place them in a recipe box for students to do after they've completed the rest of their work.

- Send the task cards home for students to complete with or without parental help.

- Provide students with designated notebooks for recording the answers to all of the task cards.

- Create a class chart, telling students to make a check mark each time they complete a task card. The first student to reach 100 wins a prize!

CONNECTION TO THE LITERARY STANDARDS

The lessons in this book support the College and Career Readiness Anchor Standards for Reading in Grades K–12. These broad standards, which serve as the basis for many state standards, were developed to establish rigorous educational expectations with the goal of providing students nationwide with a quality education that prepares them for college and careers.

Key Ideas and Details

- Refer to details and examples in a text when explaining what the text says explicitly and when drawing inferences from the text.

- Determine a theme of a story, drama, or poem from details in the text; summarize the text.

- Describe in depth a character, setting, or event in a story or drama, drawing on specific details in the text (e.g., a character's thoughts, words, or actions).

- Quote accurately from a text when explaining what the text says explicitly and when drawing inferences from the text.

- Cite textual evidence to support analysis of what the text says explicitly as well as inferences drawn from the text.

- Describe how the plot of a particular story or drama unfolds in a series of episodes as well as how the characters respond or change as the plot moves toward a resolution.

Craft and Structure

- Determine the meaning of words and phrases as they are used in a text, including those that allude to significant characters found in mythology (e.g., *herculean*).

- Compare and contrast the points of view from which different stories are narrated, including the difference between first- and third-person narrations.

- Compare and contrast two or more characters, settings, or events in a story or drama, drawing on specific details in the text (e.g., how characters interact).

- Describe how a narrator's or speaker's point of view influences how events are described.

- Explain how an author develops the point of view of the narrator or speaker in a text.

- Analyze how a particular sentence, chapter, scene, or stanza fits into the overall structure of a text and contributes to the development of the theme, setting, or plot.

Integration of Knowledge and Ideas

- Compare and contrast the treatment of similar themes and topics (e.g., opposition of good and evil) and patterns of events (e.g., the quest) in stories, myths, and traditional literature from different cultures.

Source: © Copyright 2010 National Governors Association Center for Best Practices and Council of Chief State School Officers. All rights reserved.

Literary Text

A piece of writing, such as a story or poem, that has the purpose of telling a tale or entertaining.

TIP *Before reading*, look at the title. What do you think the story will be about? *During reading*, stop and make predictions about what will happen next. Reread the parts you especially like or find confusing. *After reading*, reflect on the story. Compare it to other books and movies as well as your own life. Ask yourself, "What did the author want to tell me? What did I learn?"

Examples

- *fantasy*
- *science fiction*
- *thrillers*
- *legends*
- *folktales*
- *tall tales*
- *horror*
- *romance*
- *tragedy*
- *adventure stories*
- *friendship stories*
- *realistic fiction*
- *mysteries*
- *comedies*
- *fairy tales*
- *fables*
- *drama*
- *poems*
- *short stories*
- *plays*

Prediction

Using what you know from the text to make a smart guess about what will happen later on in a story.

TIP When you read a story, pause and play detective. Collect clues in the text and use them to make smart guesses about what will happen next. Making predictions keeps you actively engaged with the text and improves your comprehension.

Examples

- *I know that the castle is haunted, so I <u>predict</u> the main character will see a ghost.*

- *I know the wolf blew down the straw house, so I <u>predict</u> he will blow down the stick house, too.*

- *I know the main character is lonely, so I <u>predict</u> she will try to find a friend.*

- *I know the frog was a prince, so I <u>predict</u> he will turn into a prince again.*

- *I know the story takes place in a circus, so I <u>predict</u> it will be funny.*

COMPREHENSION HELPER

Inference

Drawing a conclusion about a story based on clues in the text and your own background knowledge.

TIP To make an inference, hunt for "story clues" including how characters act and what they say. Think about similar books and movies as well as your own experiences. Then, put all of that information together to make an educated guess about what is *really* going on in the story.

Examples

- *If a character has sweaty palms, you could <u>infer</u> he is nervous.*
- *If a character never speaks up in class, you could <u>infer</u> she is shy.*
- *If a character gobbles up three burgers, you could <u>infer</u> he is really hungry.*
- *If a character keeps coughing, you could <u>infer</u> she is getting sick.*
- *If a character has "a spring in his step," you could <u>infer</u> he is happy.*
- *If a character meets a magic fairy, you could <u>infer</u> she will get to make a wish.*

COMPREHENSION HELPER

Character

One of the individuals in a story. Characters are usually people, but they can also be animals or even humanized objects.

 **TIP** To better understand characters, read for details that describe them. What makes them unique? Think about what they say and do. Think about how others treat them. Think about how they are like characters in other books or like people you know. Note how they change from the first page to the last.

Examples

- *Harry Potter*
- *Percy Jackson*
- *Mary Poppins*
- *Oliver Twist*
- *Willy Wonka*
- *The Little Engine That Could*
- *Little Red Riding Hood*
- *The Big Bad Wolf*
- *The Cat in the Hat*
- *Curious George*
- *Pa Ingalls*
- *Bambi*
- *Bilbo Baggins*
- *Katniss Everdeen*
- *Greg Heffley*
- *Harriet the Spy*
- *Icarus*

Setting

The place and time in which a story happens. Settings can be realistic or fantastical. Stories can happen in the past, present, or future.

TIP To better understand a setting, read for details that tell where and when the story is happening. Compare the setting to places in your own life as well as to similar locations in other books and movies. When reading, try to form a picture in your mind so you can better "see" where and when the action occurs.

Examples

- *haunted house*
- *kid's bedroom*
- *ancient Greece*
- *New York City*
- *magic forest*
- *under the sea*
- *tree house*
- *Hogwarts School*
- *rabbit hole*
- *school*
- *Mars*
- *Alaska*
- *playground*
- *space station*
- *diner*
- *western town*
- *zoo*
- *log cabin*

Point of View

The perspective from which a story is told.

TIP Knowing who is telling a story gives you its point of view. The best way to determine a story's point of view is to investigate its pronouns. For example, if the narrator uses the pronoun *I*, that means the story is being told in the first person.

Examples

- **First Person:** *Events are told by one character, using the pronoun I. Readers step inside the character's shoes and see events only through his/her point of view.*

- **Third-Person Limited:** *Events are told through the eyes of one character using third-person pronouns such as* he *or* she. *Readers see events only from his/her point of view.*

- **Third-Person Omniscient:** *Events are told by someone outside the story, using pronouns such as* he *or* she. *This narrator can magically read everybody's mind.*

Tone

The way the narrator feels about the events, settings, and characters in a story. Tone can reveal a variety of emotions.

TIP Tone is conveyed through every part of a story including writing style, word choice, and dialogue. The best way to figure out a story's tone is to ask: *What is the narrator's attitude toward the topic, characters, and events?* The narrator's attitude sets the story's tone.

Examples

- *gloomy*
- *fantastical*
- *bossy*
- *annoyed*
- *stuck-up*
- *wise*
- *confused*
- *nervous*
- *dangerous*
- *shady*
- *warmhearted*
- *funny*
- *playful*
- *tired*
- *sincere*
- *zany*
- *enthusiastic*
- *cynical*
- *scared*
- *jealous*
- *dorky*
- *bored*
- *shy*
- *sarcastic*
- *lonely*
- *joyful*
- *mean*
- *pretentious*
- *angry*
- *witty*

Theme

The big idea or message of a story. A theme is conveyed by title, setting, and symbols. It can also be conveyed by how its characters act, learn, and change.

TIP To figure out a theme, read the whole story and ask: *How did it end? What was the author tying to tell me? How did the main characters change? What did they learn? What did I learn?* Put all your answers together. Then craft a short sentence, like the ones on the right, that clearly states the theme.

Examples

- *Be true to your own values.*
- *Family loyalty is very important.*
- *Appearances can be deceptive.*
- *Hard work builds character.*
- *Courage comes from facing down fears.*
- *True friends stick together when times get tough.*
- *Differences make people special.*
- *Happiness is contagious.*
- *Cooperation is the key to getting things done.*

COMPREHENSION HELPER

Compare and Contrast

COMPARE: To look closely at two or more things (characters, settings, plots, etc.) to see how they are similar.

CONTRAST: To look closely at two or more things to see how they are different.

TIP To compare and contrast elements of a story, be on the lookout for signal words. *Both, in common, too, also,* and *as well* relate to similarities. Words like *differ, however, only, while,* and *on the other hand* relate to differences.

Examples

- **Compare:** *The two girls were tall and athletic.*
- **Contrast:** *One girl had red hair and the other girl had black hair.*

- **Compare:** *The two settings were spooky and magical.*
- **Contrast:** *One setting was an enchanted castle and the other was a faraway planet.*

- **Compare:** *Both plots had to do with angry bullies.*
- **Contrast:** *One story had a happy ending and the other story had a sad ending.*

COMPREHENSION HELPER

Conflict and Resolution

CONFLICT: The main problem of a story.

RESOLUTION: The solution or outcome of the problem or conflict. Not all resolutions are happy ones.

TIP To locate a conflict, read the whole story; then, ask: *What went wrong? Who or what had a problem?* Words such as *problem, challenge, disagreement, trouble, unfortunately,* and *but* often signal a story's conflict. To locate a resolution, ask: *How was the conflict resolved?* Words such as *answer, result, plan, reason, solution, solve,* and *fix* often signal a story's resolution.

Examples

- **Conflict:** *A boy can't afford a new bike.*
- **Resolution:** *The boy opens a lemonade stand to raise money.*

- **Conflict:** *No one will help Little Red Hen make bread.*
- **Resolution:** *She makes the bread all by herself.*

- **Conflict:** *A family gets shipwrecked on a remote island.*
- **Resolution:** *The family builds a tree house and learns to fish.*

COMPREHENSION HELPER

Cause and Effect

CAUSE: The action or reason something happens in a story.

EFFECT: The result or consequence of that action in a story.

TIP To locate cause and effect in a story, look for relationships between actions and consequences. Play detective by starting with the *effect*. (For example, *a girl breaks her leg*.) Then backtrack through the story and locate the *cause*. (For example, *the girl falls down while skiing*.)

Examples

- **Cause:** *Lightning strikes a tree.*
- **Effect:** *The tree catches on fire.*

- **Cause:** *Jack plants a magic seed.*
- **Effect:** *A magic beanstalk grows.*

- **Cause:** *A ship crashes into an iceberg.*
- **Effect:** *The ship sinks.*

- **Cause:** *A guy eats five pizzas.*
- **Effect:** *The guy gets a stomachache.*

- **Cause:** *A wolf blows on a straw house.*
- **Effect:** *The straw house falls down.*

COMPREHENSION HELPER

Context Clues

Hints readers use to figure out the meaning of an unknown word in a text. Context clues can come before or after the unknown word.

TIP Authors use many words you may not know. But nearby words, phrases, and sentences can offer important clues to the definition of an unfamiliar word. As you read, play detective and search for clues to the mystery word's meaning. This will help improve your understanding and vocabulary without your having to reach for a dictionary.

Examples

- **Definition Clues:** *The unknown word is defined in the text.*
- **Example Clues:** *An example of the unknown word is provided in the text.*
- **Synonym Clues:** *A word with a similar meaning is near the unknown word.*
- **Antonym Clues:** *A word with the opposite meaning is near the unknown word.*

Text Evidence

Exact words, phrases, or sentences in a text that provide information, answer a question, or support a claim.

TIP When citing text in a story, frame your text evidence with a sentence stem such as, *According to the text*. Follow that with a comma or colon. Then place the <u>exact words</u> from the text in quotation marks. (See examples at right.)

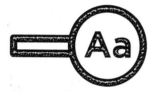

Examples

- *According to the text, "Sarah was upset because her pet parrot flew away."*
- *An example of alliteration in the text is, "Fifteen falcons flew to Florida."*
- *The author states: "The castle was dark, gloomy, and filled with the ghosts of old gladiators."*
- *A sentence that compares the two pets is, "Karl's dog was a sleek and confident Great Dane, while Lisa's dog was a cute and cuddly mutt."*
- *The story says, "The temperature dipped down to 20 below."*

Figurative Language

Words and phrases that mean something different from what the words actually say.

TIP Figurative language keeps writing fresh and surprising. If you are reading along and encounter words and phrases that don't seem to mean what they say, chances are you've encountered figurative language. Check out some examples in the box at the right.

Examples

- **Similes:** *Two things compared using* like *or* as, *e.g., as big as a whale.*
- **Metaphors:** *Two things compared NOT using* like *or* as, *e.g., her eyes were two priceless jewels.*
- **Personification:** *Objects or animals that act like humans, e.g., the wind howled.*
- **Hyperbole:** *Exaggerated phrases, such as my throat was as dry as the Sahara desert.*
- **Onomatopoeia:** *Words that sound like what they mean, such as buzz and sizzle.*
- **Alliteration:** *Repeated use of the same beginning sound for a poetic effect, e.g., lovely lilacs are luxurious.*

100 LITERARY TASK CARDS

LITERARY TEXT: PREDICTION

What's Going On?

Maddie woke up on Saturday feeling **jubilant**. It was her 12th birthday. But then something weird happened: Nobody mentioned it. Her mom said, "Good morning, Sugarplum!" the way she always did. Her brother ignored her and kept eating his cereal. When Maddie phoned Lia, her best friend, Lia didn't even call her back! That was odd. Later, Maddie went to her violin lesson, just like every other Saturday. This, she thought, was the worst birthday ever! But then, as Maddie was returning home, she saw Lia going in her front door. And her friend, Stella, too. And why were there bunches of balloons out front? What was going on?

KEY QUESTIONS

1. PREDICTION: What do you think happens next in the story?

2. PREDICTION: Do you think Maddie will still consider this the worst birthday ever? Why?

3. INFERENCE: Why doesn't her mom say "Happy Birthday" to Maddie?

4. CONTEXT CLUES: What do you think *jubilant* means?

☐ thrilled
☐ tired
☐ fearful

5. S-T-R-E-T-C-H: How does the story end? Complete it.

LITERARY TEXT: PREDICTION

Opposite Robot

Dr. Mavis Morkus built herself a robot. Right away, she noticed something was wrong. She asked the robot to nod its head "yes." The robot shook its head "no." She asked the robot to stay still. The robot broke into a silly dance. *Hmmmm.* This robot always seemed to do the opposite of what it was told. So Dr. Morkus had a bright idea. Her laboratory was a big mess. Cleaning it up was one of her least favorite tasks. "Robot," said Dr. Morkus, "I **command** you *not* to clean up my lab."

KEY QUESTIONS

1. PREDICTION: What do you think happens next in the story?

2. PREDICTION: If Dr. Morkus wanted the robot to sleep, what would she tell it to do?

3. TEXT EVIDENCE: What does the robot do when it's told to stay still? Cite the text.

4. CONTEXT CLUES: What do you think *command* means?

☐ compute
☐ order
☐ dance

5. S-T-R-E-T-C-H: What would you like an opposite robot to do? What would you say to it?

LITERARY TEXT: PREDICTION

Homework Headache

Mario always did his homework, without fail. But his friend Derrick wasn't as **conscientious**.  Derrick always *meant* to do his homework, but then he'd start playing a new video game and lose track of time. One morning Derrick asked Mario if he could copy his homework so he would get a good grade on the assignment. Mario knew it was a bad idea, but he agreed anyway. The next day, their teacher asked both Mario and Derrick to stay after school to discuss "a serious problem involving them both." Mario felt bad because he thought that Derrick was going to get in trouble. It did not occur to him that he might be in trouble, too.

KEY QUESTIONS

1. PREDICTION: What do you think will happen next in the story?

2. PREDICTION: Do you think Mario is right that only Derrick will get in trouble? Why?

3. CHARACTER: Can you describe Derrick in a sentence or two?

4. CONTEXT CLUES: What do you think *conscientious* means?

☐ impatient
☐ friendly
☐ hardworking

5. S-T-R-E-T-C-H: Why do you think Mario agreed to let Derrick copy his homework? Was that wise?

LITERARY TEXT: PREDICTION

Planet Wingding

Wingding has to be one of the strangest planets in the universe. It looks pretty much like Earth, but there is one major difference. On Wingding, every creature can fly. Cities are filled with flying people. I was shocked the first time I saw a flying boy with a flying dog on a leash. But things got even more **bizarre** when I visited a farm. While walking around, I heard a loud "moo" above me. I looked up to see a cow standing in a giant tree.  The cow spread its huge spotted wings and leapt off the branch.

KEY QUESTIONS

1. PREDICTION: What do you think happens next in the story?

2. PREDICTION: What other unusual winged creatures might the narrator see on the farm?

3. COMPARE AND CONTRAST: How are planets Earth and Wingding alike? How are they different?

4. CONTEXT CLUES: What do you think *bizarre* means?

☐ very small
☐ very strange
☐ very expensive

5. S-T-R-E-T-C-H: Imagine you see one of Wingding's flying animals. Describe it.

LITERARY TEXT: PREDICTION

Flying High

Meg was terrified of heights, but she wanted to **vanquish** her fear once and for all. So, she signed up for trapeze school. When she saw the trapeze bar, 20 feet in the air, a small voice in her head said, "*No way!*" But Meg politely told that voice, "*Yes way.*" The teacher strapped her in a harness. "You can't fall," he reminded her. Meg nodded. As she climbed the ladder, she started to sweat and her inner voice whispered, "*No way.*" But when she got to the top, she calmly declared, "*Yes way,*" and she grabbed hold of the trapeze bar.

KEY QUESTIONS

1. PREDICTION: What do you think happens next in the story?

2. PREDICTION: How do you think Meg will feel at the end of her lesson?

3. INFERENCE: How does Meg feel when she's climbing the ladder?

4. CONTEXT CLUES: What do you think *vanquish* means?

- ☐ love
- ☐ fall
- ☐ beat

5. S-T-R-E-T-C-H: Have you ever conquered a fear? Tell about it.

LITERARY TEXT: PREDICTION

Baking Cookies

Natalie loved to bake! So, she asked her grandma if she could make cookies. "Sure," her grandma said, "but remember to keep an eye on them so they don't burn." Natalie measured the ingredients and mixed them together. She spooned **dollops** of cookie dough onto a cookie sheet and set the kitchen timer for 15 minutes, just as she'd seen her grandma do. She couldn't wait to eat them. Her tummy growled in anticipation. Natalie went into the den to watch TV. The TV was so loud, she didn't hear the timer when it beeped.

KEY QUESTIONS

1. PREDICTION: What do you think will happen next in the story?

2. PREDICTION: How do you think Natalie's grandma will respond?

3. TEXT EVIDENCE: Why doesn't Natalie hear the timer go off? Cite the text.

4. CONTEXT CLUES: What do you think *dollops* means?

☐ cups   ☐ blobs   ☐ dozens

5. S-T-R-E-T-C-H: An *onomatopoeia* is a word that sounds like its meaning, such as *kaboom*. Can you find two examples in this story? Use them both in original sentences.

LITERARY TEXT: PREDICTION

Sharing Sherice

Sherice bought a mini-pizza and sat down to eat it. Her friend, Lisa, said that she was hungry, so Sherice split her pizza with her. Another time, Sherice purchased two bottles of nail glitter at the store. Lisa said that she **adored** nail glitter, so Sherice gave her one of the bottles. At the amusement park, Sherice had two tickets left to go on rides. She'd already gone on all the single-ticket rides, like the teacup and Ferris wheel. She was looking forward to the big roller coaster, which cost two tickets. "Darn it!" announced Lisa, "I just ran out of tickets."

KEY QUESTIONS

1. PREDICTION: What do you think happens next in the story?

2. PREDICTION: What might Lisa say if she knew Sherice had two packs of gum?

3. CHARACTER: Can you describe Sherice's character in a sentence or two?

4. CONTEXT CLUES: What do you think *adored* means?

☐ needed
☐ loved
☐ hated

5. S-T-R-E-T-C-H: What things do you share with your friends? Tell about them.

LITERARY TEXT: PREDICTION

A Day at the Beach

Matt had red hair and fair skin. Like everyone in his family, he burned when he was out in the sun too long. One summer, his family decided to spend a few days at the beach. Matt had never seen the ocean before. Swimming in the sea and searching for shells was fun. His favorite activity, though, was building a gigantic sand castle. The sun was bright, so his mom reminded him to **slather** on lots of sunscreen. But Matt was having such a blast that he completely forgot to do it.

KEY QUESTIONS

1. PREDICTION: Do you think Matt will end up with a sunburn?

2. PREDICTION: What clues in the story helped you make your prediction?

3. TEXT EVIDENCE: What was Matt's favorite beach activity? Cite the text.

4. CONTEXT CLUES: What do you think *slather* means?

☐ crawl quickly
☐ swim slowly
☐ spread thickly

5. S-T-R-E-T-C-H: What lesson do you think Matt will learn from his day at the beach?

Lucy's Odd Luck

It was Friday the 13th, a day famous for bad luck. And what a day Lucy was having! First, she broke her hand mirror. That was supposed to bring seven years of bad luck. Instead, her grandmother surprised her with seven freshly baked cookies. Then, some men were working on the building next door. Lucy walked under their ladder. Walking under a ladder is also supposed to bring bad luck. But Lucy soon found a crisp ten-dollar bill! After that, Lucy crossed paths with a large black cat. Black cats  are a well-known **harbinger** of bad luck. But you'll never guess what happened next!

KEY QUESTIONS

1. PREDICTION: What do you think happens next in the story?

2. PREDICTION: Do you think Lucy's odd luck will continue on Saturday the 14th? Why or why not?

3. DETAILS: How many cookies does Lucy's grandmother bake for her?

4. CONTEXT CLUES: What do you think *harbinger* means?

☐ secret
☐ sign
☐ pet

5. S-T-R-E-T-C-H: Why do you think the story is called *Lucy's Odd Luck*?

Six Scoops

Mark was in the mood for ice cream. He asked for one scoop of chocolate and one scoop of vanilla, as well as one scoop each of strawberry, peach, mint, and rainbow. Six scoops! Carefully, he opened the door of the sweet shop. Mark was now carrying a cone with a very tall and very **precarious** stack of ice cream scoops. Slowly, he walked to the park. Two people were throwing a Frisbee back and forth. Suddenly, the Frisbee came flying straight at Mark's arm . . . . *Yikes!*

KEY QUESTIONS

1. PREDICTION: What do you think happens next in the story?

2. PREDICTION: Can you think of a fun story twist where Mark doesn't lose his ice cream? Share it.

3. DETAILS: What six ice cream flavors are on Mark's cone?

4. CONTEXT CLUES: What do you think *precarious* means?

☐ tall
☐ delicious
☐ likely to fall

5. S-T-R-E-T-C-H: *Yikes!* Use this word in a brand-new sentence.

LITERARY TEXT: INFERENCE

Where's Dinner?

"What's for dinner?" Kyle asked Mom. Their big dog, Zeke, jumped up **exuberantly**. He understood the word *dinner*. Mom told Kyle they were having hamburgers, and she asked him to take the ground beef out of the refrigerator while she made a quick phone call. Kyle did as his mother asked and then went to finish his homework. "Kyle!" Mom called when she returned to the kitchen. "I thought I asked you to take the meat out of the fridge." He pointed to the counter, where he'd put the hamburger, but it was gone. "Hey, where did it

go?" Kyle asked, puzzled.

"Wait a minute!" Mom said. "Where's Zeke???"

KEY QUESTIONS

1. INFERENCE: What do you think happened to the meat?

2. INFERENCE: Why does Mom say, "Where's Zeke?"

3. PREDICTION: What do you think will happen next in the story?

4. CONTEXT CLUES: What do you think *exuberantly* means?

☐ nervously
☐ harshly
☐ excitedly

5. S-T-R-E-T-C-H: Can you think of another title for this story?

LITERARY TEXT: INFERENCE

The Favor

Zoe had been excited about the field trip to the zoo, so when she got sick and couldn't go, she felt **dispirited**. Her pal Luke came by to borrow her cell phone. "Mine's broken," he said. "You won't need yours since you'll be home tomorrow."

The next day, Zoe thought about all the fun she was missing. Then Luke came by to return her phone. "I took a couple of pictures," he said with a smile.

"Wow!" shouted Zoe. Her phone was filled with lots of new photos, including pictures of a lion, zebra, and giraffe!

"Thanks, Luke," she said. "I almost feel like I was there."

KEY QUESTIONS

1. INFERENCE: What favor does Zoe do for Luke? What favor does Luke do for Zoe?

2. INFERENCE: Why does Zoe say, "I almost feel like I was there"?

3. CHARACTER: What kind of friend is Luke? How do you know?

4. CONTEXT CLUES: What do you think *dispirited* means?

☐ happy
☐ sad
☐ silly

5. S-T-R-E-T-C-H: Have you done a special favor for a friend? Tell about it.

Up a Tree

My cousin Juan always had to be the best at everything. One day, he and I were climbing the big maple tree in my yard. I'd been climbing that tree ever since I was little. I knew every branch **like the back of my hand**, but Juan had never climbed a tree before. Even so, he kept climbing higher and higher. When he passed me by, he said he wasn't scared. He just kept climbing higher. When he finally stopped and looked down, he began to cry. He couldn't move. We had to call the fire department to get him down!

KEY QUESTIONS

1. INFERENCE: Why does Juan keep climbing higher?

2. INFERENCE: Why does the fire department have to be called?

3. DETAILS: How are Juan and the narrator related?

4. CONTEXT CLUES: What do you think the saying *like the back of my hand* means?

☐ very well
☐ not very well
☐ very joyful

5. S-T-R-E-T-C-H: Do you think Juan learned a lesson? What was it?

The Big Night

Ava quietly practiced her lines one last time: "To be or not to be. That is the question." She gathered with the other fifth graders backstage, and Ms. Lee told them to keep their voices down. "We've got a big audience!" Ms. Lee said excitedly. Ava's wool costume made her arms itch, but she was too nervous to care. She always had the **jitters** before she went on stage. But once she got going, she knew she'd be fine. The whole class had been rehearsing for weeks. They were ready to knock 'em dead!

KEY QUESTIONS

1. INFERENCE: Why is Ava practicing her lines?

2. INFERENCE: Has Ava been in performances before? How do you know?

3. SETTING: Where is this story set?

4. CONTEXT CLUES: What do you think *jitters* means?

☐ questions
☐ memories
☐ nervous feelings

5. S-T-R-E-T-C-H: What do you think *knock 'em dead* means? Use this saying in a new sentence.

Ty's Jeans

Twelve-year-old Ty wore his faded old jeans nearly every day. The jeans were his favorite piece of clothing. They fit him just right, and they were soft and comfortable. But when summer came, he put the jeans away and pulled out a pair of shorts. Ty lived in Texas, and he and his friends wore shorts from May to September. When the weather cooled, he pulled his favorite jeans out of the chest of drawers, but he discovered something **peculiar**. His pants were too short!

KEY QUESTIONS

1. INFERENCE: Why does Ty pull out his jeans when the weather turns cool?

2. INFERENCE: Why are Ty's jeans too short for him in September?

3. DETAILS: What state does Ty live in?

4. CONTEXT CLUES: What do you think *peculiar* means?

☐ annoying
☐ strange
☐ old

5. S-T-R-E-T-C-H: Do you have a favorite article of clothing? Describe it.

Mystery of the Muddy Footprints

Young Deer, Dog, and Duck were the best of friends. This was surprising, since they were all such different creatures. But they were on the same soccer team. They also liked pop music and video games. One day, the three friends were playing outside after a giant rainstorm. They were soon **drenched** and covered in mud. Mrs. Deer called them to come inside for a snack. Two of the friends wiped their feet clean on the doormat, but one left a trail of muddy footprints. The prints were from a pair of webbed feet. "Who tracked mud into my home?" asked Mrs. Deer.

KEY QUESTIONS

1. INFERENCE: Who tracked mud into Mrs. Deer's home?

2. INFERENCE: What are the clues that led you to your suspect?

3. TONE: Is this story silly or serious? How do you know?

4. CONTEXT CLUES: What do you think *drenched* means?

☐ very happy
☐ very hungry
☐ very wet

5. S-T-R-E-T-C-H: What happens next in the story? Come up with an ending.

The Birthday Breakfast

Dan wanted to make his mom breakfast on her 38th birthday. It had to be pancakes, piled high with maple syrup! That was her favorite. He got up at 6:30, and got to work. When everything was ready, he **summoned** his mom to the table. She smiled with delight when she saw what Dan had done. When his mom took her first bite she said, "*Mmmm!* The best pancakes I've ever had!" But when Dan took a bite, he  realized the pancakes tasted terribly salty. He must have read the recipe wrong. But his mom looked super happy as she ate the pancakes anyway.

KEY QUESTIONS

1. INFERENCE: Why do you think Dan's mom says these are the best pancakes she's ever had?

2. INFERENCE: Do you think Dan's mom can taste the salt in the pancakes?

3. DETAILS: How old is Dan's mother?

4. CONTEXT CLUES: What do you think *summoned* means?

☐ arranged
☐ called
☐ cleared

5. S-T-R-E-T-C-H: Have you ever done something special for a family member's birthday? Tell about it.

Fly Away Home

I was looking for a place to rest. I landed on this girl's scarf. Her scarf was the same pattern as my shell. It was **scarlet** with black dots. I figured I would stay there for a while. I was feeling snug as a bug in a rug. Then, the girl noticed me. She tried to flick me off with her finger. She missed. But I know when I'm not wanted. I flew away and landed on a quiet, green leaf. I took a nice long nap where nobody could bother me. After that, I had a nice snack of little green bugs called aphids. *Munch, crunch!*

KEY QUESTIONS

1. INFERENCE: What kind of creature is this story about?

2. INFERENCE: What is a clue that makes clear what the creature is?

3. POINT OF VIEW: Who is the narrator of this story?

4. CONTEXT CLUES: What do you think *scarlet* means?

☐ red
☐ black
☐ bright

5. S-T-R-E-T-C-H: What do you think the saying *snug as a bug in a rug* means? Use it in a sentence.

LITERARY TEXT: INFERENCE

Cherry Lemonade

It was a bright summer day. Brad set up a sidewalk stand. He was selling lemonade and cherry ice pops. "I'll have one of each," said his first customer. As he handed the customer the ice pop, Brad noticed that the package was full of liquid. Right then, Brad had an **inspiration**. "Would you like to try cherry lemonade instead," he asked?

"That sounds refreshing," said the customer. Brad poured the package into a glass of lemonade. He stirred it with a spoon. Turns out, the cherry lemonade was delicious. Soon there was a long line at his stand.

KEY QUESTIONS

1. INFERENCE: What was the weather like this day?

2. INFERENCE: What happened to the cherry ice pops?

3. TEXT EVIDENCE: How do you know Brad's creation was popular? Cite the text.

4. CONTEXT CLUES: What do you think *inspiration* means?

☐ lots of sweat
☐ another silly idea
☐ sudden brilliant idea

5. S-T-R-E-T-C-H: Think of an advertising slogan for Brad's drink creation.

LITERARY TEXT: INFERENCE

Go Fly a Kite

On Saturday, Sania put on her sweater and went out to fly her kite. The kite soared way up high. What fun! On Sunday, she decided to do the same activity. But this time, her experience was very different. Whenever Sania took off running, the kite would rise just as it had the day before. But it would only stay up for a few seconds before **hurtling** back down to the ground. *Oh well*, thought Sania, *there will be other days to fly a kite*. Instead, she decided to jump in a freshly raked pile of leaves.

KEY QUESTIONS

1. INFERENCE: In what season does this story take place? How do you know?

2. INFERENCE: Why won't Sania's kite stay up in the air?

3. TEXT EVIDENCE: What does Sania do instead of flying her kite? Cite the text.

4. CONTEXT CLUES: What do you think *hurtling* means?

☐ moving very slowly
☐ moving quickly and wildly
☐ moving in a circle

5. S-T-R-E-T-C-H: What is your favorite season and why?

LITERARY TEXT: CHARACTER

A New Home

One day, Tam saw her neighbor Mrs. Simon putting the trash out on the curb. She noticed that Mrs. Simon was throwing away a plant, along with a bag of trash. The plant was growing in a little green pot. It was crooked and yellowish, with just a few little leaves. Tam felt sorry for the plant, out there on the curb waiting to be hauled away. She decided to rescue it. Both Tam and her mom had **a green thumb** and loved to garden, so they brought the plant into their backyard and gave it a new home in the dirt.

KEY QUESTIONS

1. CHARACTER: Can you describe Tam in a sentence or two?

2. CHARACTER: How does Tam differ from Mrs. Simon?

3. INFERENCE: Is the plant healthy or not? How do you know?

4. CONTEXT CLUES: What do you think the saying *a green thumb* means?

☐ very ill
☐ good with plants
☐ good at art

5. S-T-R-E-T-C-H: What do you think will happen to the plant in its new home? Why?

LITERARY TEXT: CHARACTER

The Late Leaf

It was November. Every leaf in the woods had fallen—every leaf, that is, except for a single oak leaf. It didn't **budge**. The other leaves on the ground called out, "Come down and play." Even the tree told the late leaf to go. But the worried leaf held on. It hated change. Suddenly, a mighty wind blew, and the leaf had no choice. Down it fell. At first, the leaf was nervous. But then it started to flip, float, and fly. "This is fun!" said the leaf.

"We told you so!" shouted the other leaves from below.

KEY QUESTIONS

1. CHARACTER: Can you describe the leaf's character in a sentence or two?

2. CHARACTER: Why is this leaf called the "late leaf"?

3. FIGURATIVE LANGUAGE: *Alliteration* is a sequence of words that start with the same letter, such as "dance, dip, and dive." Can you find an alliteration in the story?

4. CONTEXT CLUES: What do you think *budge* means?

☐ float   ☐ turn brown   ☐ move

5. S-T-R-E-T-C-H: What do you think happens when the leaf hits the ground? Create an ending.

To Go or Not to Go?

When Max's mom told him that he was invited to Jackson's birthday party, he sighed. *Oh, no*, he thought. *A party*. Jackson was a new friend, and it was nice of him to invite Max. But none of Max's other friends would be there. The party would be filled with kids Max didn't know at all! The idea of a bunch of strangers made him nervous.

"You always have fun at parties," his mom reminded him. "It just takes you a little while to **warm up**."

Max thought about this and realized something: She was right!

KEY QUESTIONS

1. CHARACTER: Can you describe Max in a sentence or two?

2. CHARACTER: How does Max feel about meeting new people?

3. INFERENCE: Why is the title *To Go or Not to Go?*

4. CONTEXT CLUES: What do you think the saying *warm up* means?

☐ get hot
☐ get comfortable
☐ get hungry

5. S-T-R-E-T-C-H: Do you think Max goes to the party? Tell why you think so.

A Girl Called N.V.

N.V. is what everyone called Niki Veronica. Besides being her initials, her nickname was perfect because she was so full of **envy**. Whenever someone had something, N.V. always wanted it. Jan got a new bracelet. N.V. wanted it. Jabir got a pet fish. N.V. wanted it. Alison got a cool yo-yo. N.V. wanted it.

But then Danny got chicken pox. "I want it," said N.V.

This was just plain weird. So Sammi asked: "Do you even know what chicken pox is?"

"It's food right, like nuggets?" replied N.V.

"No, it's an illness," explained Sammi. "Trust me, N.V., even *you* don't want chicken pox!"

KEY QUESTIONS

1. CHARACTER: Can you describe N.V.'s character in a sentence or two?

2. CHARACTER: Why did the author use the initials N.V.?

3. PREDICTION: What would N.V. do if another kid got a skateboard?

4. CONTEXT CLUES: What do you think *envy* means?

☐ goofiness
☐ happiness
☐ jealousy

5. S-T-R-E-T-C-H: Briefly describe a character named Gary Oswald whose initials are G.O.

No Bones for You

Whenever Toby the sheepdog got a new bone, he buried it in the backyard. One day his buddy Baxter hopped over the fence to play. Toby **crowed** about how many bones he had. One by one, he dug them up to show Baxter. There must have been fifteen or twenty. Baxter's humans never gave him bones. He asked if he could have just one of the bones, but Toby snarled, "These are mine!" Baxter said that if he had that many bones, he would happily share them with Toby. "I guess that's the difference between you and me," Toby barked.

KEY QUESTIONS

1. CHARACTER: Can you describe Toby in a sentence or two?

2. CHARACTER: How do you think Toby's actions make Baxter feel?

3. TEXT EVIDENCE: What does Toby do when he gets a new bone? Cite the text.

4. CONTEXT CLUES: What do you think *crowed* means?

☐ lied
☐ bragged
☐ screamed

5. S-T-R-E-T-C-H: Imagine you are a dog. Would you rather be friends with Toby or with Baxter? Why?

Waiting for the Bus

Olivia waited, shivering, at the bus stop. It had just started to snow, and she'd forgotten her coat. She couldn't wait to get inside the nice, warm bus. She looked up the street every minute or two, and felt relieved when she finally saw the bus. Just then an old woman approached. The woman was bent over and **frail**, and she leaned on a walker. Olivia thought how hard it must be for the woman to get around, especially in cold weather. When  the bus doors opened, Olivia moved aside and let the old woman get on first. Then she helped the woman find a seat.

KEY QUESTIONS

1. CHARACTER: Can you describe Olivia in a sentence or two?

2. CHARACTER: How does Olivia feel about the old woman?

3. INFERENCE: What season is it in the story? How do you know?

4. CONTEXT CLUES: What do you think *frail* means?

☐ cold
☐ weak
☐ uncomfortable

5. S-T-R-E-T-C-H: Do you think Olivia is someone you'd like to be friends with? Why?

José's Favorite Subject

After Mr. Morgan handed back the spelling tests, most of the fifth graders were upset. The whole class had done poorly. All except for José, who got an A+. José *always* got great grades,  and he made sure everyone knew it. "That test was **a piece of cake**!" he bragged to Anita as they walked to the cafeteria. "And you know what's really funny? I didn't even study! I was too busy playing soccer. Did you hear I scored four goals? We won because of me!" José was so busy talking that he didn't notice Anita had walked away.

KEY QUESTIONS

1. CHARACTER: Can you describe José in a sentence or two?

2. CHARACTER: What is José's favorite subject to talk about?

3. INFERENCE: Why do you think Anita walks away when José is talking?

4. CONTEXT CLUES: What do you think the saying *a piece of cake* means?

☐ hard
☐ hungry
☐ easy

5. S-T-R-E-T-C-H: What advice would you give José?

Zany Zelda

Our parents told us to dress nicely. We were going out to dinner. My sister, Zelda, **donned** a pretty green dress, but that was not all. She also wore a bright blue wig and a red clown nose. No one could ever tell Zelda what to do. During dinner, she turned her back to me for a moment. When she whirled around, she'd put two carrots in her mouth like fangs. Soon she was wearing an onion ring on her wrist  like a bracelet. She slurped her milk through ten straws. When the waiter came around, Zelda announced, "Now I'm ready for some dessert."

KEY QUESTIONS

1. CHARACTER: Can you describe Zelda's character in a sentence or two?

2. CHARACTER: Why is this story titled *Zany Zelda*?

3. PREDICTION: What happens next in this story? Share your idea.

4. CONTEXT CLUES: What do you think *donned* means?

☐ put on
☐ washed
☐ made

5. S-T-R-E-T-C-H: Would you like to have dinner with Zelda? Why or why not?

Donnie at the Dentist

Donnie did not like going to the dentist one bit. The moment he sat in the chair, a feeling of **dread** washed over him. So he decided to think about other things. Donnie pictured himself as an explorer deep in the rain forest. A bird landed on the windowsill outside the dentist's office. *What would it be like to be a bird?* wondered Donnie. He pictured himself flying high above the city. Next, he saw himself flying in a rocket. The rocket landed on Neptune. Neptune was crawling with orange octopus creatures. "All finished," said the dentist.

   "Wow, that went fast!" said Donnie with a grin.

KEY QUESTIONS

1. CHARACTER: Can you describe Donnie's character in a sentence or two?

2. CHARACTER: How does Donnie deal with an unpleasant situation like going to the dentist?

3. INFERENCE: Why does Donnie grin at the end?

4. CONTEXT CLUES: What do you think *dread* means?

☐ joy
☐ fear
☐ cavities

5. S-T-R-E-T-C-H: What's something Donnie might imagine during a boring car trip? Share it.

Marvin Starts His Day

Beep, beep, beep! "Where was that sound coming from?" wondered Marvin. Then, he crawled under his bed, found his alarm clock, and turned it off. Then he got dressed. His only clean shirt was in his pants drawer. His clean pants were **draped** over his drum set. Then Marvin went downstairs for breakfast. He spilled cornflakes on the counter. He dribbled orange juice on the table. He dropped bacon on the floor. Then he walked out the door, across the lawn, through a puddle, and off to school.

KEY QUESTIONS

1. CHARACTER: Can you describe Marvin's character in a sentence or two?

2. CHARACTER: What might work well as a different title for this story?

3. DETAILS: What three things did Marvin have for breakfast?

4. CONTEXT CLUES: What do you think *draped* means?

☐ arranged loosely
☐ carefully folded
☐ freshly ironed

5. S-T-R-E-T-C-H: What do you think happens on Marvin's walk to school? Tell about it.

Big Score, Small Prize

Lights flashed. *Ding, ding, ding* went the bells on dozens of games played by dozens of kids. Omar pushed the button again and again as fast as he could. The elf on his screen jumped over a toadstool and crawled under a rainbow. *Ring, ring, ring* went his machine. Omar had just scored one million points, a new high score! The machine spit out a long row of tickets. Bursting with pride, Omar **ambled** over to a prize counter.

   "What can I buy with these?" asked Omar.

   "For all those tickets, you can get either a comb or a pencil eraser," responded the man at the counter.

KEY QUESTIONS

1. SETTING: Where does this story take place?

2. SETTING: Does this story take place long ago or in current times? How do you know?

3. FIGURATIVE LANGUAGE: *Personification* is when an object behaves like a person. Can you find an example in the story?

4. CONTEXT CLUES: What do you think *ambled* means?

☐ ran
☐ walked
☐ flew

5. S-T-R-E-T-C-H: What does the story's title mean? Explain it.

After Hours

All the visitors had gone home for the day. That's when a painting called *Myrna Lucy* got the fun started. During regular hours, she was a **somber** portrait of an unsmiling woman. Now she crossed her eyes and shouted, "Party time!" A portrait called *Prince Gregory* put on giant sunglasses. And another painting called *The Sad Clown* started to giggle and blow up balloons. Suddenly, a guard's shoes could be heard clicking toward them. He peeked in the room: silence. All the paintings had gone back to normal. The guard continued down the hall. *Myrna Lucy* stuck out her tongue, and the fun began again.

KEY QUESTIONS

1. SETTING: Where does this story take place?

2. SETTING: When does this story take place? How do you know?

3. TEXT EVIDENCE: What item does *Prince Gregory* put on? Cite the text.

4. CONTEXT CLUES: What do you think *somber* means?

☐ funny
☐ irritable
☐ serious

5. S-T-R-E-T-C-H: Describe another painting and how it might behave in this situation. Don't be afraid to get silly!

Seeing the Sights

During the short break from school, Charlotte went to visit her favorite aunt. The weather was just starting to turn warm, and they spent two days seeing the sights. They went to the White House, the Capitol, and the National Gallery of Art. But Charlotte's favorite sight was the Lincoln Memorial, with its **majestic** statue of Abraham Lincoln. The 19-foot sculpture of President Lincoln was made of white marble. The other highlight wasn't a

 building or monument. It was the magnificent cherry trees with their bright pink blossoms that had just begun to bloom. Beautiful!

KEY QUESTIONS

1. SETTING: In what city does this story take place?

2. SETTING: What time of year is it in the story? What clue helped you figure it out?

3. DETAILS: What sights does Charlotte see on her trip?

4. CONTEXT CLUES: What do you think *majestic* means?

☐ marble
☐ magical
☐ grand

5. S-T-R-E-T-C-H: What would you like to see if you visited this city? Tell why.

Did You Hear That?

Cal **nudged** his older brother Stanley, who was snoring like a buzz saw in his sleeping bag. "Stanley! Did you hear that?" Stanley opened one eye and looked at Cal in the dark tent. "Something was rustling outside," Cal whispered. "Maybe it's a bear. Maybe it's going to eat us." Stanley groaned. "It's NOT a bear! Go back to sleep." But Cal couldn't sleep. He heard the sound again. Very slowly, he unzipped the tent. He saw his dad taking out the trash. Then his dad went back in the house. "Phew," Cal sighed. Soon he was out like a light.

KEY QUESTIONS

1. SETTING: Where does this story take place?

2. SETTING: What time of day is it in the story?

3. CHARACTER: Can you describe Cal in a sentence or two?

4. CONTEXT CLUES: What do you think *nudged* means?

☐ heard
☐ whispered
☐ poked

5. S-T-R-E-T-C-H: A simile compares two unlike things using the word *like* or *as*. *Sleep like a log* is a simile. Can you find two in the story?

Time for Broccoli

Broccoli lived in a bin next to his fellow vegetables. He could see shoppers walking in the aisle. He could see the sun shining through the front window.  Broccoli knew he wasn't the most popular item. He could see carts piled high with bread, apples, and eggs. One day, a woman reached into the vegetable bin. She was holding a grocery list, and "carrots" was not yet marked off. Broccoli **summoned** all his power to send the woman a silent message. "YOU NEED BROCCOLI."

"*Hmmmm,*" said the woman. "I don't think I'll get carrots after all."

She picked up Broccoli. He'd been chosen!

KEY QUESTIONS

1. SETTING: Where does this story take place?

2. SETTING: Does it take place during the day or during the night? How do you know?

3. DETAILS: The woman chooses broccoli instead of what item?

4. CONTEXT CLUES: What do you think *summoned* means?

- ☐ whispered
- ☐ laughed
- ☐ called upon

5. S-T-R-E-T-C-H: Describe your favorite vegetable in detail.

The Lion's Roar

 Pamela's four-year old brother, Owen, was driving her crazy. "I want to see the lions!" he kept screaming. But the lions were on the opposite side of the park, so he had to wait. It was a bright summer day, and they saw giraffes and elephants and chimpanzees. But Owen wasn't interested. "I want to see the lions!" he said for the ten thousandth time. Finally, they arrived where the lions were. They spotted a huge male **slinking** along a grassy slope. The lion looked right at them and let out a ferocious roar. "Aaaagh!" Owen screamed. "We need to leave right now!"

KEY QUESTIONS

1. SETTING: Where does this story take place?

2. SETTING: What is the weather like in the story? How do you know?

3. FIGURATIVE LANGUAGE: A *hyperbole* is an exaggerated statement, such as, *this weighs a ton.* Can you find one in this story? Try!

4. CONTEXT CLUES: What do you think *slinking* means?

- ☐ eating loudly
- ☐ moving quietly
- ☐ crying slowly

5. S-T-R-E-T-C-H: Why does Owen want to leave when they finally see a lion?

The Trip Home

Ryan sat in his seat and stared out the window. It had been a great trip to Los Angeles. He was now on his way back home to Boston. He looked out the window. The sky was dark blue and dotted with stars. A flight attendant came by and collected what was left of his dinner. Then a voice came over the loudspeaker. It was the pilot, announcing that they had begun their **descent.** They would be landing soon. Ryan

knew the sound of that voice better than anyone. The pilot was his mom. Ryan looked at his dad and smiled with pride.

KEY QUESTIONS

1. SETTING: Where does this story take place?

2. SETTING: Does this story take place during the day or at night? How do you know?

3. TEXT EVIDENCE: Where does Ryan live? Cite the text.

4. CONTEXT CLUES: What do you think *descent* means?

☐ movement downward
☐ spinning motion
☐ movement upward

5. S-T-R-E-T-C-H: Why does Ryan smile with pride?

A Perfect Sand Castle

The school year was over. The sun was shining, and it was 85 degrees. Waves crashed on the shore. Henry and his brother Ozzy built a giant sand castle with seventeen tall towers. Then they stepped back to **admire** their creation. It was perfect! But the next morning, when they went to see their castle, it had disappeared. "Oh, no! It's gone," said Henry sadly.

"Don't worry," said Ozzy. "We'll rebuild the exact same sand castle in the exact same spot." And so they did.

KEY QUESTIONS

1. SETTING: Where does this story take place?

2. SETTING: What season is it? How do you know?

3. INFERENCE: Why did their sand castle disappear?

4. CONTEXT CLUES: What do you think *admire* means?

☐ view with pleasure
☐ laugh at
☐ swim near

5. S-T-R-E-T-C-H: What do you predict will happen to the new sand castle? What advice would you give these boys about sand castle–building?

What a Catch!

Kesha and her granddad had great seats! She'd already **devoured** a hot dog and munched peanuts from a little bag. And their team was ahead 4 to 2. Under the bright lights, she watched their pitcher throw strike after strike. Kesha beamed at her granddad. A minute later, there was a loud *crack*, and then the ball was whizzing up into the stands. In fact, it was heading . . . straight for Kesha and her granddad! Her granddad always brought his mitt to games, and without thinking twice, he reached out his arm and caught the ball, just like a pro!

KEY QUESTIONS

1. SETTING: Where does this story take place?

2. SETTING: What time of day is it in the story? What clue helped you?

3. INFERENCE: How does Kesha feel about her granddad? How do you know?

4. CONTEXT CLUES: What do you think *devoured* means?

- [ ] grilled
- [ ] eaten slowly
- [ ] eaten quickly

5. S-T-R-E-T-C-H: An *onomatopoeia* is a word that sounds like its meaning, such as *kerplunk*. Can you find two in this story? Use each in a sentence.

Floating Toothpaste

Through the window, I could see Earth. It looked like a blue marble. I undid my seat belt. Soon I was floating around completely weightless. *Wheeeee!* I did some cartwheels and flips. But there was important work to do, too. I set the necessary controls and recorded some **vital** scientific measurements. Then I remembered that I hadn't brushed my teeth since before liftoff. I squeezed some toothpaste from its tube, and it hung in midair. I tried to catch it, but that little blue squiggle 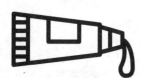 floated away. *Hee-hee!* Who would have thought brushing my teeth would be such a challenge?

KEY QUESTIONS

1. SETTING: Where does this story take place?

2. SETTING: How does the view through the window give a clue to the setting?

3. INFERENCE: Is this narrator silly, serious, or both? How do you know?

4. CONTEXT CLUES: What do you think *vital* means?

- [ ] nutritious
- [ ] ridiculous
- [ ] important

5. S-T-R-E-T-C-H: What happens next? Finish the story.

Three Birthdays in One

Lia, Tia, and Pia were triplets. Their 11th birthday was in just a few days. Lia wanted to spend the day at a nearby amusement park, riding roller coasters and eating corn dogs. She thought that would be the most fun birthday ever. Tia **loathed** this idea. She thought amusement parks were SO overrated. She wanted to spend the day at the beach, splashing in the waves. Pia didn't like either of these ideas. She wanted to go to an ice cream shop and get a milkshake. That, she thought, would be the perfect birthday. Which plan did their parents end up choosing? All three! They went to an amusement park in the morning, the beach in the afternoon, and an ice cream shop at night.

KEY QUESTIONS

1. POINT OF VIEW: Which characters' minds can the reader "see" into?

2. POINT OF VIEW: What point of view is this story told in?

☐ first person
☐ third-person limited
☐ third-person omniscient

3. DETAILS: What does Lia want to do for their birthday?

4. CONTEXT CLUES: What do you think *loathed* means?

☐ loved ☐ hated ☐ agreed with

5. S-T-R-E-T-C-H: Which of the triplets' birthday ideas would you choose? Why?

Humpty Dumpty: The Truth

I'm Father Goose. I'd like to offer a different **perspective** on a famous tale. Humpty Dumpty was neither sitting on a wall, nor did he have a great fall. He was playing soccer. He tried to bounce the ball off his head—and *CRACK*! Now, let's discuss the part about all the king's horses and all the king's men. Why would such a large group be required to put Humpty together again? Truly, all it took was a single doctor to fix Humpty's shell. I watched the whole thing. Of course, my wife, Mother Goose, tells a different story. But she has a very lively imagination.

KEY QUESTIONS

1. POINT OF VIEW: Who is the narrator of this story?

2. POINT OF VIEW: What point of view is this story told in?

☐ first person
☐ third-person limited
☐ third-person omniscient

3. TEXT EVIDENCE: In this version of the story, how did Humpty crack his shell?

4. CONTEXT CLUE: What do you think *perspective* means?

☐ point of view ☐ path
☐ suggestion

5. S-T-R-E-T-C-H: Use your imagination to tell what really happened in another nursery rhyme story.

The Magic Show

"We need a volunteer from the audience," the magician loudly **bellowed**. Guess whose hand shot up. Mine—I'm Melvin Gelby. In a flash, I was up on the stage. The truth is, I'd always wanted to be in a magic act. I wanted to think of a secret number, and then have the magician guess what it was. In fact, I had a number ready: 10,654,982,773. It would have to be a pretty good magician to figure out that one! But the magician didn't ask me to think of a number. Instead, he told the audience that he was going to saw me in half. *Gulp!*

KEY QUESTIONS

1. POINT OF VIEW: What is the narrator's name?

2. POINT OF VIEW: What point of view is this story told in?

☐ third-person omniscient
☐ first person
☐ third-person limited

3. DETAILS: What number does the narrator have ready?

4. CONTEXT CLUE: What do you think *bellowed* means?

☐ believed   ☐ worried   ☐ shouted

5. S-T-R-E-T-C-H: How does the story end? Finish it.

Allie Gets Her Own Room

Allie's family was moving to a new house. Allie had just one burning question: Who would get the bigger bedroom? Allie and her sister, Iris, shared a room, but in the new house they would each get their own room. Iris said she should get the bigger room because she was older. But Allie thought that was unfair. It wasn't *her* fault she was born two years after Iris. She thought *she* should get it because Iris was **domineering** and always got her way. When Allie finally saw the new house, she breathed a sigh of relief. The two bedrooms were exactly the same size!

KEY QUESTIONS

1. POINT OF VIEW: Which character's mind can the reader "see into"?

2. POINT OF VIEW: What point of view is this story told in?

☐ first person   ☐ third-person limited
☐ third-person omniscient

3. INFERENCE: Why is Allie relieved at the end of the story?

4. CONTEXT CLUES: What do you think *domineering* means?

☐ sly   ☐ bossy   ☐ generous

5. S-T-R-E-T-C-H: If one of the bedrooms were bigger, which sister do you think should get it? Why?

Trader Tom

I traded a piece of gum for a marble. I played with the marble for a while, then I traded it for a comic book. I had read the entire comic book, so I traded it for an action figure. I enjoyed the action figure for a while, then traded it for a bike. I rode the bike around for a few hours, then I traded it for two pieces of gum. That might sound like an **absurd** trade, but here's how I figure it. I'll chew one piece of gum. I'll trade the other piece and start working my way back to another bike.

KEY QUESTIONS

1. POINT OF VIEW: Can you figure out the narrator's name?

2. POINT OF VIEW: What point of view is this story told in?

☐ first person
☐ third-person limited
☐ third-person omniscient

3. DETAILS: What does the narrator trade the comic book for?

4. CONTEXT CLUES: What do you think *absurd* means?

☐ clever   ☐ expensive   ☐ silly

5. S-T-R-E-T-C-H: Do you think the narrator will reach his goal of a bike? Tell why.

Banana Peel Boy to the Rescue

Frog Girl could jump high. Tiger Lady could run fast. But Banana Peel Boy was not much of a superhero. He wore a slippery yellow suit and sat around Superhero Headquarters all day reading comic books. But then, an evil **villain** named Cheetah Man came to town to cause trouble. Cheetah Man was so fast that even Tiger Lady couldn't catch him. Finally, Banana Peel Boy took action. He lay down on the sidewalk and waited for Cheetah Man to run by. *Slip . . . Klunk!* Cheetah Man fell down and was carted off to jail. At long last, Banana Peel Boy was a superhero.

KEY QUESTIONS

1. POINT OF VIEW: Can you tell what any of the characters is thinking?

2. POINT OF VIEW: What point of view is this story told in?

☐ first person   ☐ third-person limited
☐ third-person omniscient

3. CONFLICT AND RESOLUTION: Cheetah Man's quickness is the problem. What is the resolution?

4. CONTEXT CLUES: What do you think *villain* means?

☐ good guy   ☐ bad guy   ☐ small town

5. S-T-R-E-T-C-H: Imagine and describe a brand-new superhero.

Ugh! Braces!

"Braces!" Suki screamed. "My life is over!" Fifth grade was hard enough, she thought. The last thing she needed was a mouthful of metal. Her mom thought Suki was **making a mountain out of a molehill**. She remembered when she had braces when she was a girl. After the first couple of weeks, she'd forgotten all about them. "Just think of the perfectly straight teeth you'll have in two years," she told Suki. "TWO YEARS??" Suki wailed.

   Suki's best friend, Ben, thought Suki's reaction was perfectly reasonable. He knew exactly how she felt. *Exactly.* That's because he just found out that he needed braces, too!

KEY QUESTIONS

1. POINT OF VIEW: What characters' minds can the readers "see" into?

2. POINT OF VIEW: What point of view is this story told in?

☐ third-person omniscient
☐ first person ☐ third-person limited

3. INFERENCE: Why does Suki say her life is over?

4. CONTEXT CLUES: What do you think the saying *making a mountain out of a molehill* means?

☐ new ☐ worried ☐ exaggerating

5. S-T-R-E-T-C-H: Use the saying *making a mountain out of molehill* in a brand-new sentence.

The Sixth-Grade Champ

I'm Linda Breen. In third grade, I came in second in the class spelling bee. In fourth grade, I came in second, and in fifth grade I came in second. All three years, I lost to Jamal Porter. The next year, I was determined to win! I printed lists of words and had my little brother quiz me every night. On the day of the spelling bee, I felt like a spelling superhero. I **slew words like dragons**. Finally, it was down

to just Jamal and me. He got the word *condescension,* and he left out the second *c.* Then it was my turn, and I spelled it like a c-h-a-m-p!

KEY QUESTIONS

1. POINT OF VIEW: What is the narrator's name?

2. POINT OF VIEW: What point of view is this story told in?

☐ first person ☐ third-person limited
☐ third-person omniscient

3. INFERENCE: Who won the spelling bee? How do you know?

4. CONTEXT CLUES: What do you think the saying *slew words like dragons* means?

☐ spelled words badly
☐ spelled words well
☐ became a creature

5. S-T-R-E-T-C-H: What's the hardest word you know how to spell? Spell it and give its meaning.

Just Chillin'

Today's my first day of summer break. I played some basketball. I drank a cherry slush. It gave me the most **intense** brain freeze ever. I caught a lizard and climbed up in a tree house. I dribbled my new basketball and then went for a swim. It was the first time I ever worked up the nerve to jump off the high-dive board. Next, I rode my bike. I had a second slush. This one was lime. It didn't give me a brain freeze. I watched puppies for a while through a pet store window. Later, I ran into my friend, Teddy. "What's up?" asked Teddy. "Not much," I said with a relaxed smile. "Just chillin'."

KEY QUESTIONS

1. POINT OF VIEW: Even though you don't know this character's name, what are some things you'd guess about this person?

2. POINT OF VIEW: What point of view is this story told in?

☐ first person ☐ third-person limited
☐ third-person omniscient

3. DETAILS: What was the flavor of this character's second slush?

4. CONTEXT CLUES: What do you think *intense* means?

☐ anxious ☐ cold ☐ very powerful

5. S-T-R-E-T-C-H: What do you like to do when you're just chillin'?

Puffed-up Pete

Pete the puffer fish loved to think about himself! Pete thought about his braininess. He got great grades at the school of fish. Pete thought about his skill at sports. He had just won a swimming contest. Then Pete thought about how handsome and hilarious he was. Pete kept thinking until he was nearly bursting with pride. *Poof!* Pete puffed up into a big round spiky ball. Then Pete let himself **deflate**. He kept deflating until he was back to a regular-looking fish. What did all the other fish think? They thought Pete was a lot easier to be around when he wasn't so puffed up with his own importance.

KEY QUESTIONS

1. POINT OF VIEW: Can you tell what Pete is thinking? Can you tell what the other fish are thinking?

2. POINT OF VIEW: What point of view is this story told in?

☐ first person
☐ third-person limited
☐ third-person omniscient

3. CAUSE AND EFFECT: What causes Pete to puff up?

4. CONTEXT CLUES: What do you think *deflate* means?

☐ get tired ☐ let air out
☐ swim fast

5. S-T-R-E-T-C-H: Would you like to be pals with Pete? Why or why not?

Not-So-Blue Monday

Brrrring! goes my lousy alarm clock. Time to get up. Did I mention that I **detest** Mondays? First, I get dressed. Man, these clothes are uncomfortable. Next, Mom tells me to brush my teeth. How can a toothbrush be so bristly? Then I eat breakfast. *Yuck!* These cornflakes are soggy. Now, I'm on the bus. The view out the window is always the same: boring! Now, I'm walking into my school. Why are other kids so noisy? Now, I'm sitting down at my desk. This chair is too low. Here comes my teacher handing back papers. *Hmmmm*, I got an *A*. Okay, that is . . . totally spectacular! I guess Mondays can be pretty awesome after all.

KEY QUESTIONS

1. TONE: What is the main tone of this story?

☐ happy ☐ scary ☐ cranky

2. TONE: Does the tone of the story change at the end? Why?

3. INFERENCE: Why do you think the author chose the title *Not-So-Blue Monday*?

4. CONTEXT CLUES: What do you think *detest* means?

☐ hate ☐ love ☐ forget

5. S-T-R-E-T-C-H: What's something that could change your mood from bad to good? Tell about it.

I'm the Best!

Some people in my class think math is hard. I guess not everyone can be as smart as I am, but I don't see what they find so difficult. Math is a snap! And when some people complain about all the homework our teacher gives us, I just roll my eyes. Maybe if they were as smart as I am, it wouldn't take them so long to finish! Luckily, I'm so brilliant that I can finish my homework really fast. That leaves me plenty of time to hang out with friends. I don't really have any friends, though. I think I must **intimidate** people!

KEY QUESTIONS

1. TONE: What is the tone of this story?

☐ sad ☐ boastful ☐ playful

2. TONE: Do you think this tone makes the narrator seem likable? Tell why.

3. INFERENCE: Why do you think the narrator doesn't have any friends?

4. CONTEXT CLUES: What do you think *intimidate* means?

☐ make angry ☐ make nervous
☐ make sleepy

5. S-T-R-E-T-C-H: What advice would you give this narrator to make more friends?

Missing Scooter

I remember the day I saw the sign in front of Scooter's house across the street: *For Sale*. "Is it true?" I asked him in worried barks. Scooter was a mutt just like me, and my best friend. We played together in the park every day, splashing in puddles and fetching balls. He nodded **mournfully**. Yes, it was true. His humans were moving. A few weeks later, I sat on my front porch and watched Scooter's family pack up the car. He waved his furry

paw and hopped into the backseat. After that, the car drove away. Good-bye forever, best buddy!

KEY QUESTIONS

1. TONE: What is the tone of this story?

☐ whimsical ☐ sad ☐ hopeful

2. TONE: How does the narrator feel about Scooter moving away?

3. INFERENCE: Who is the narrator of this story?

4. CONTEXT CLUES: What do you think *mournfully* means?

☐ sadly ☐ joyfully ☐ quickly

5. S-T-R-E-T-C-H: What happens next in the story? Share it.

At the Snail Races

Hi! Sally Sporter here. If you've just tuned in on your TV, this is incredible! Snail #1, with the tan shell, is in the lead. Snail #2, with the white shell, is close behind. They are nearing the finish line. Oh, my! Snail #1 has stopped. Snail #2 is still moving forward. Now Snail #2 is in the lead. What blinding speed! What **determination**! Snail #2 is crossing the finish line. Snail #2 is the winner! This is amazing, folks! I've never seen a more exciting snail race. Tune in next week for the turtle high jump.

KEY QUESTIONS

1. TONE: What is the tone of this story?

☐ sad ☐ serious ☐ silly

2. TONE: How would you describe Sally Sporter?

3. DETAILS: What color is Snail #2's shell?

4. CONTEXT CLUES: What do you think *determination* means?

☐ really slow
☐ strong-willed
☐ super fast

5. S-T-R-E-T-C-H: What do you think a turtle high jump competition would be like? Use your imagination to describe it.

The Shadowy Figure

For the first time, Jose was spending the night at his grandmother's. She lived in a dark, old house on a lonely hill. That evening, in his room, Jose heard this sound! *Creak!* Someone was on the stairs. He was pretty sure his grandmother had gone to bed. So who—or what—was it? The doorknob started to turn back and forth. Jose's hair stood on end. Then the old door swung open. *Screeeeech*. A shadowy figure stood there. "Hello, Jose," said the shadowy figure. "I couldn't sleep, so I baked you some sugar cookies."

It was just Grandma! And her cookies were **scrumptious**.

KEY QUESTIONS

1. TONE: What is the tone of this story?

☐ hopeful ☐ spooky ☐ proud

2. TONE: How does the setting of the story contribute to the tone?

3. FIGURATIVE LANGUAGE: An *onomatopoeia* is a word that sounds like its meaning, such as *splat*. Can you find two examples in this story? Try!

4. CONTEXT CLUES: What do you think *scrumptious* means?

☐ delicious ☐ terrifying out
☐ homemade

5. S-T-R-E-T-C-H: Describe a situation where you got scared, but it turned out to be nothing.

Fast Friends

Kim frowned. It was her first day at a new school, and she didn't know anybody. During class, she sat quietly at her desk. The teacher didn't even seem to notice her. At lunch, Kim sat by herself. All the other kids were talking and giggling. Kim felt like the most friendless girl in the whole universe. Then it was time for gym. The kids were running races. Fortunately, Kim happened to be an **extraordinarily** fast runner. By the end of gym, Kim smiled. She'd made a bunch of new friends!

KEY QUESTIONS

1. TONE: What is the tone at the beginning of the story?

☐ excited ☐ lonely ☐ boastful

2. TONE: How did the tone change at the end of the story? Why?

3. FIGURATIVE LANGUAGE: A *hyperbole* is an exaggeration, such as "He has a million toys." Can you find one in this story? Try!

4. CONTEXT CLUES: What do you think *extraordinarily* means?

☐ especially ☐ blandly
☐ normally

5. S-T-R-E-T-C-H: What are some things you can do to make a new kid in school feel welcome? Share your ideas.

The Worst Day Ever

Last Thursday was the worst day of my life. I was in the cafeteria, eating with some older kids that I didn't know very well. We were having a nice time until one of them said, "Hey Mike, what's all over your face?" *Aagh!* It was mustard from my sandwich! And then, as if that weren't bad enough, when I got up from my seat, I tripped and fell! *Splat!* The plate in  my hand went flying through the air and then landed with a loud smack. Everyone turned to look. I was **mortified**! I'll never get over it in a million years!

KEY QUESTIONS

1. TONE: What is the tone of this story?

☐ embarrassed ☐ happy ☐ proud

2. TONE: Do you think this really was the worst day of Mike's life? Tell why.

3. FIGURATIVE LANGUAGE: An *onomatopoeia* is a word that sounds like its meaning, such as *beep*. Can you find two examples in this story? Try!

4. CONTEXT CLUES: What do you think *mortified* means?

☐ hungry ☐ frightened
☐ embarrassed

5. S-T-R-E-T-C-H: Do you think Mike will really *never* get over his embarrassment? Tell why.

Babysitting

When my dad said I had to babysit my little sister, I was not pleased. "Oh, *great*," I said with a fake smile. "In fact, there's nothing I'd rather do!" My sister was a huge **nuisance**. She cried all the time. She was such a little genius that she did brilliant things like sticking a lima bean in her nose. When she ate, more of the food ended up on her face than in her mouth. It was just *beautiful!* You can see why I loved hanging out with her soooooo much! My dad said I did some crazy stuff when I was little, too, but I *highly* doubt it.

KEY QUESTIONS

1. TONE: What is the tone of this story?

☐ sarcastic ☐ admiring ☐ excited

2. TONE: Does the narrator mean it when he or she says, "In fact, there's nothing I'd rather do!"?

3. INFERENCE: Why do you think the narrator's sister gets food on her face when she eats?

4. CONTEXT CLUES: What do you think *nuisance* means?

☐ pest ☐ comfort ☐ friend

5. S-T-R-E-T-C-H: What else do you think this narrator would say about his or her sister? Finish the story.

Tortoise Time

Tortoise heard humans walking in the woods. So he **retracted** his head and legs into his shell. He waited. Then he heard some chittering chipmunks. So he waited a little longer. Finally, they went away. He started to stick out his head. *Wait, what was that?!* Oh, it was a bird squawking. At last the bird left, and the woods seemed safe. Tortoise carefully stuck out his head. Slowly, he stretched out his feet from his shell and started to walk. Gee, it sure had been a dangerous afternoon.

KEY QUESTIONS

1. TONE: What is the tone of this story?

☐ energetic ☐ nervous ☐ angry

2. TONE: Is this story exaggerated? Why do you think so?

3. TEXT EVIDENCE: What scares tortoise at the beginning of the story? Cite the text.

4. CONTEXT CLUES: What do you think *retracted* means?

☐ pull in ☐ wiggle ☐ jump

5. S-T-R-E-T-C-H: What happens next in the story? End it.

My Baby Brother

When the new baby came, I was furious. How could they do this to me? For the past six years, I had been their princess! Their pride and joy! When I took my first steps, they cheered! Talk about crazy. How hard is it to walk? And when I learned to use a fork? They went nuts! They **cherished** my every move. But then my little brother showed up. And suddenly *he* began getting all the attention. All I can say is, this stinks! I wanted to get really mad at the little guy. But I just couldn't. He's too darn cute.

KEY QUESTIONS

1. TONE: What is the tone of this story?

☐ disliked ☐ adored ☐ laughed at

2. TONE: What is the narrator's attitude toward her baby brother?

3. INFERENCE: In the story, who are "they?"

4. CONTEXT CLUES: What do you think *cherished* means?

☐ hated ☐ adored ☐ photographed

5. S-T-R-E-T-C-H: What else might this narrator say about her baby brother? Write a few more lines.

Extreme Burger

Tim and Theo were having lunch at Burger Barn. Tim ordered a regular hamburger. "A plain burger? That is so boring!" scoffed Theo.

Then Theo ordered the Extreme Burger. It had four beef patties, mushrooms, onions, bacon, and pineapples. The whole thing was covered in sour cream, hot mustard, and secret sauce. When the Extreme Burger arrived, it was as big as a spaceship. Theo took a bite. *Yuck!* It tasted **ghastly**! So Tim offered Theo half of his burger. Theo gladly accepted. *Mmmmm.* A plain old hamburger never tasted better!

KEY QUESTIONS

1. THEME: What is the theme of this story?

☐ Friends should share burgers.
☐ Fancy isn't always better.

2. THEME: What lesson do you think Theo learns?

3. FIGURATIVE LANGUAGE: A *hyperbole* is an exaggeration, such as "This book weighs a ton." Can you find one in this story?

4. CONTEXT CLUES: What do you think *ghastly* means?

☐ delicious ☐ spooky ☐ horrible

5. S-T-R-E-T-C-H: Can you think of another example in which the fanciest choice isn't the best choice?

The Myth of King Midas

The god Dionysus granted King Midas a single wish. Immediately the king knew what to ask for. He asked that everything he touched would turn to gold. Gold, gold, gold! He would be the richest person on earth! The god agreed and granted King Midas his wish. But soon, the king realized he'd made a terrible mistake, and that his wish was actually a curse. Everything he touched—food, drink, even his young daughter—*every single thing* he touched turned to solid gold. He begged the god to

free him from this terrible curse, and Dionysus agreed. Happily, the king's daughter was **restored** to flesh and blood.

KEY QUESTIONS

1. THEME: What is the theme of this story?

☐ Being greedy can get you into trouble.
☐ Having lots of gold is great.

2. THEME: What lesson do you think King Midas learns?

3. CHARACTER: How would you describe the king at the start of the story?

4. CONTEXT CLUES: What do you think *restored* means?

☐ cursed ☐ forgiven ☐ returned

5. S-T-R-E-T-C-H: Why was the king's wish really a curse?

A Change of Plans

When Jen turned fourteen, her parents said she could start babysitting to earn some money. Not long after, Ms. Miller, who lived next door, called and asked if Jen could babysit that Friday. Ms. Miller and her husband had tickets to a play. Jen jumped at the chance. But then on Thursday, Jen's friend Alissa invited her to a concert on Friday night. Jen really wanted to go, so she called Ms. Miller and told her that she couldn't babysit after all. Ms. Miller sounded **irked** and said she wished Jen had let her know sooner. Ms. Miller never asked Jen to babysit after that.

KEY QUESTIONS

1. THEME: What is the theme of this story?

☐ When you go back on your word, people won't trust you.
☐ Doing what you want is always the best choice.

2. THEME: What lesson do you think Jen learns?

3. CHARACTER: What word would you use to describe Jen?

4. CONTEXT CLUES: What do you think *irked* means?

☐ pleased ☐ loud ☐ annoyed

5. S-T-R-E-T-C-H: If you were going to give Jen some advice, what would it be?

Zack's Sax

The first time Zack blew into his saxophone, it made an awful sound. His sax sounded like an old hound dog howling at the moon. The next day, he tried again. There wasn't much improvement. Now, Zack's sax sounded like a car screeching to a **halt**. He thought about giving up. But he decided to keep practicing. The next day he sounded a little better. The day after that, he sounded better still. One day, after a few months of practice, he picked up his sax and blew into it. Wow! Now Zack's sax sounded, well, perfect. Maybe he'd even join a jazz band.

KEY QUESTIONS

1. THEME: What is the theme of this story?

☐ Practice makes perfect.
☐ Music makes everyone happy.

2. THEME: What lesson did you learn from this story?

3. FIGURATIVE LANGUAGE: A simile compares two unlike things using the word *like* or *as*. *Sparkled like diamonds* is a simile. Can you find two similes in this story?

4. CONTEXT CLUES: What do you think *halt* means?

☐ stop ☐ ear ☐ fast

5. S-T-R-E-T-C-H: Describe an activity you got better at with practice.

The Ants and the Grasshopper

At the end of summer, the ants began preparing for the long, cold winter ahead. Their friend the grasshopper **serenaded** them as they worked, singing songs and playing the fiddle. At first the ants enjoyed the grasshopper's lighthearted attitude. But then they began to worry. They reminded him that winter was coming and there wouldn't be any food. He'd better start preparing. But the grasshopper just wanted to sing and play and enjoy himself. When winter arrived, the grasshopper had nothing to eat, and he nearly starved. The ants felt sorry for him and shared their food. At last the grasshopper understood why they had warned him to prepare.

KEY QUESTIONS

1. THEME: What is the theme of this fable?

- [ ] Work hard and be prepared.
- [ ] Be joyful in everything you do.

2. THEME: What lesson do you think the grasshopper learns?

3. TEXT EVIDENCE: What does the grasshopper want to do? Cite the text.

4. CONTEXT CLUES: What do you think *serenaded* means?

- [ ] sang to [ ] made fun of
- [ ] argued with

5. S-T-R-E-T-C-H: Are you more like the ant or the grasshopper? Why?

All You Can Chew

Clara loved bubble gum. Whenever she saw a machine, she would drop in a quarter and get a gumball. *Chomp, chomp!* Then she'd blow a big bubble. *Pop!* On her twelfth birthday, Clara unwrapped a big box. It was her very own gumball machine! She didn't need quarters anymore. Clara kept turning the knob, getting gumball after gumball. Soon her mouth was filled with a huge gum glob. She chewed until her jaw hurt. She tried to blow a bubble. *Snap!* The bubble bust all over her face. It even got in her hair! That's when Clara **resolved** to stick to one gumball at a time.

KEY QUESTIONS

1. THEME: What is the theme of this story?

- [ ] You can have too much of a good thing.
- [ ] It is wise to give thoughtful gifts.

2. THEME: What lesson do you think Clara learns?

3. FIGURATIVE LANGUAGE: An *onomatopoeia* is a word that sounds like its meaning. Can you find three examples in the story?

4. CONTEXT CLUES: What do you think *resolved* means?

- [ ] strongly chewed [ ] strongly breathed
- [ ] strongly decided

5. S-T-R-E-T-C-H: Write an imaginary public-service message warning people not to chew too much gum at once.

The Boy Who Cried Wolf: An Aesop's Fable

There once was a shepherd boy whose job was to sit on the hillside and watch the sheep. It was a boring job. One day, he got fed up. He wanted something interesting to happen. What did the boy do? He raced into the village shouting, "Wolf! Wolf!" The villagers came running, assuming the flock was in **jeopardy**. But they soon realized the boy had tricked them and there was no wolf. A few days later, the boy did the same thing, and again everyone came running. Again, they realized they'd been tricked. The next day there actually *was* a wolf, but when the boy ran into the village for help, everyone ignored him.

KEY QUESTIONS

1. THEME: What is the theme of this fable?

☐ When you lie a lot, people won't believe you when you tell the truth.
☐ Hard work is its own reward.

2. THEME: What lesson do you think the shepherd boy learns?

3. TEXT EVIDENCE: Why does the boy say there's a wolf when there isn't one? Cite the text.

4. CONTEXT CLUES: What do you think *jeopardy* means?

☐ wool ☐ hunger ☐ danger

5. S-T-R-E-T-C-H: What do you think the saying "cry wolf" means? Why is it a bad thing to do?

Best Friends

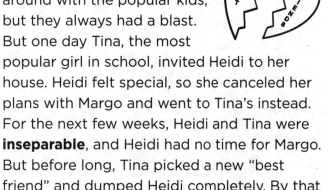

Heidi and Margo were best friends. They didn't hang around with the popular kids, but they always had a blast. But one day Tina, the most popular girl in school, invited Heidi to her house. Heidi felt special, so she canceled her plans with Margo and went to Tina's instead. For the next few weeks, Heidi and Tina were **inseparable**, and Heidi had no time for Margo. But before long, Tina picked a new "best friend" and dumped Heidi completely. By that time, Margo had started hanging out with the new girl in school, Lydia. Poor Heidi, she really ruined a good thing.

KEY QUESTIONS

1. THEME: What is the theme of this story?

☐ Always try to make new friends.
☐ Always be loyal to your true friends.

2. THEME: What lesson do you think Heidi learns?

3. DETAILS: What is the name of Heidi's new best friend?

4. CONTEXT CLUES: What do you think *inseparable* means?

☐ always sleeping ☐ always fighting
☐ always together

5. S-T-R-E-T-C-H: The story ends: "Poor Heidi, she really ruined a good thing." What does that mean?

A Little Surprise

It was Manny's birthday and he was so excited to open his gifts. He started with the biggest box, of course! Inside was a giant pillow! What a **massive** disappointment! Next, he opened a tiny box to which he hadn't paid any mind. It contained a slip of paper with numbers: 38-1-21. Turns out, it was the combination to a lock. Yes, locked up in front of Manny's house was a brand-new bike with a big red ribbon on it. It was the best gift ever!

KEY QUESTIONS

1. THEME: What is the theme of this story?

- ☐ No one wants a pillow for a gift.
- ☐ Great gifts can come in small packages.

2. THEME: What lesson do you think Manny learns?

3. DETAILS: What numbers were on the slip of paper?

4. CONTEXT CLUES: What do you think *massive* means?

☐ fluffy ☐ cheap ☐ huge

5. S-T-R-E-T-C-H: Describe a big gift that could come in a small package.

The Acrobat and the Apples

Larry was the ringmaster of the circus. Walking home one day, he saw an apple tree. He jumped up and down, but couldn't reach an apple. Larry **fancied** himself the star of the circus. He never wanted anyone's help. The next day, he returned to the apple tree. He tried jumping again. That's when Zazi spotted him. She was an acrobat at the same circus.

"Let me help you," she said. Quick as a wink, Zazi climbed up on Larry's shoulders. She picked two apples from the tree—one for each of them. *Yum, yum!*

KEY QUESTIONS

1. THEME: What is the theme of this story?

- ☐ Sometimes it's a good idea to ask for help.
- ☐ An apple a day keeps the doctor away.

2. THEME: What lesson do you think Larry learns?

3. TEXT EVIDENCE: What is Larry's circus skill? Cite the text.

4. CONTEXT CLUES: What do you think *fancied* means?

☐ thought ☐ frilly ☐ dressed

5. S-T-R-E-T-C-H: Use your imagination to describe a situation that might require three acrobats.

The Great Brownie Bake-off

In Treatville, people loved brownies. No one ate candy or cookies, *ever*. It was brownies or nothing. But there was a bit of a **controversy** in town. Some thought Beth Baker's brownies were the best. Others believed Dan Delish's brownies couldn't be beat. So they decided to have a bake-off. The town's mayor, Fred Foodie, would judge. Beth's brownies were small and gooey. Dan's were big and cakey. But both types of brownies were sweet and chocolatey. On the big day, the mayor wolfed down 100 brownies in total before declaring the bake-off . . . a delicious tie!

KEY QUESTIONS

1. COMPARE: How are Beth's and Dan's brownies similar?

2. CONTRAST: How are they different?

3. DETAILS: How many brownies does the mayor eat?

4. CONTEXT CLUES: What do you think *controversy* means?

☐ disagreement
☐ prize
☐ decision

5. S-T-R-E-T-C-H: Is this story realistic? Tell why or why not.

No Place Like Home

Mina loves living in the city. When she looks out her window, she sees skyscrapers above and yellow taxi cabs below. She loves the hustle and bustle and all the people on the streets. Her cousin Padma hates noise and crowds. She loves living in the **suburbs**, where it's quiet. She's surrounded by lawns and trees and one-story houses. When Mina's mom asks the girls if they'd want to trade places,

both cousins have the same reply: *No way!* They both love their homes and couldn't imagine living anywhere else.

KEY QUESTIONS

1. COMPARE: How are Mina's and Padma's opinions similar?

2. CONTRAST: How are their opinions different?

3. DETAILS: What does Mina see from her window?

4. CONTEXT CLUES: What do you think *suburbs* means?

☐ areas outside the city
☐ big cities
☐ farms

5. S-T-R-E-T-C-H: Would you rather live in a city or a suburb? Why?

Scaredy Monsters

Todd the Troll and Gwen the Goblin were best friends. They both had cuddly teddy bears. They both loved sunny beaches and hated dark caves. But they had some differences, too. Todd's favorite food was cupcakes. Gwen's favorite food was rice pudding. Todd loved the sound of birds chirping. Gwen **preferred** the sound of opera singing. One day, there was a knock at the door. They both went to answer. It was Wilma the Werewolf. "*Aaaaaaaah!*" they screamed together. That's another thing Todd and Gwen had in common: They were both scaredy monsters.

KEY QUESTIONS

1. COMPARE: How are Todd and Gwen similar?

2. CONTRAST: How are they different?

3. INFERENCE: Why do you think Todd and Gwen hate dark caves?

4. CONTEXT CLUES: What do you think *preferred* means?

☐ showed off fangs
☐ liked better
☐ disliked

5. S-T-R-E-T-C-H: Use your imagination and write more ways Todd and Gwen are alike and different.

Strongman Versus Ant

The strongman lifted a 500-pound weight. The crowd roared. Now it was the ant's turn. The ant lifted a half-ounce cheese curl. The people responded with surprise and silence. But there was a little crowd of ants watching, too. They let out a tiny roar.

"I declare this contest a tie," said the judge. "The strongman lifted a heavy weight. But a cheese curl is equally heavy for a tiny ant."

The strongman was **impressed**, too. He leaned down and, with his huge hand, he shook each of the ant's six tiny legs.

KEY QUESTIONS

1. COMPARE: How are the strongman and ant similar?

2. CONTRAST: How are they different?

3. TEXT EVIDENCE: How much did the strongman lift? Cite the text.

4. CONTEXT CLUES: What do you think *impressed* means?

☐ respectful
☐ tiny
☐ strong

5. S-T-R-E-T-C-H: What's a man vs. creature contest you'd like to see? Why?

Postcards From Camp

Lucy got postcards from her two best friends, Aisha and Ella. They were away at camp. She read Aisha's note first. *Hi Lu: Adventure camp is awesome! I'm learning a lot. We've been rock climbing and swimming. One day we even went white-water rafting. I never want to leave!*

Then she read Ella's letter. *Hey Lucy-Goosey: Theater camp is great! I'm learning a lot. I'm starring in the camp play, and tonight is our big show. It's been super fun, but exhausting. I'm ready to get home and chill.*

Lucy was glad her friends were having fun. And she was **elated** they'd be home soon!

KEY QUESTIONS

1. COMPARE: How are Aisha's and Ella's camp experiences similar?

2. CONTRAST: How are they different?

3. DETAILS: What two nicknames do Lucy's friends call her?

4. CONTEXT CLUES: What do you think *elated* means?

- ☐ jealous
- ☐ very happy
- ☐ worried

5. S-T-R-E-T-C-H: Would you rather go to Lucy or Aisha's camp? Explain why.

What Pet Should We Get?

Glen and his mom were talking about what kind of pet to get. His mom told Glen that both cats and dogs need to be fed every day. *And given care and attention.* Then she told him that unlike cats, dogs need to go for walks daily. And some dogs get lonely if they're left alone too long. Glen thought about the fact that he'd be at school all day, and his mom would be at work. His mom said that cats are less **social** and don't mind being on their own.

"I think we should get a cat," Glen said.

KEY QUESTIONS

1. COMPARE: How are dogs and cats similar?

2. CONTRAST: How are they different?

3. PREDICTION: What do you think happens next in the story?

4. CONTEXT CLUES: What do you think *social* means?

- ☐ likes to be outside
- ☐ likes to eat
- ☐ likes to be around others

5. S-T-R-E-T-C-H: What pet would you rather have? Tell why.

Pen Pals

"I'm a bird," wrote Puffin to Penguin, her pen pal. "I like to eat fish. I am little. I can fly. I live near the North Pole. It is cold here."

"I'm a bird, too," wrote Penguin to Puffin. "I also like to eat fish. I am big. I can waddle. I live near the South Pole, where it is cold. Hey, let's meet somewhere warm."

So the two pen pals picked the perfect place. They decided to meet in the tropics, an equal **journey** for each. It was perfect because Puffin and Penguin both loved palm trees.

KEY QUESTIONS

1. COMPARE: How are Puffin and Penguin similar?

2. CONTRAST: How are they different?

3. FIGURATIVE LANGUAGE: Alliteration is a sequence of words that start with the same letter, such as "An icy igloo near Iceland." Can you find one in the story?

4. CONTEXT CLUES: What do you think *journey* means?

☐ a trip
☐ a webbed foot
☐ an ocean

5. S-T-R-E-T-C-H: What happens when the two birds meet? Finish the story.

Who's Scared?

Will was terrified of roller coasters. Even looking at a roller coaster, racing and dipping, going a million miles an hour, sent him into a panic. When he heard his friend Lynne talking about how awesome the Super-Duper Quadruple Corkscrew was, he felt **envious**. He wished he could be daring and brave like Lynne. But Lynne wasn't completely fearless. The first time she saw Will's pet snake, she screamed. "Aren't you afraid to sleep in the same room as a snake?" she asked.

"Nah," Will said. "Snakes are cool!" At that moment, Will realized that Lynne had fears, too—just like him.

KEY QUESTIONS

1. COMPARE: How are Will and Lynne similar?

2. CONTRAST: How are they different?

3. INFERENCE: Why does Lynne scream when she sees Will's snake?

4. CONTEXT CLUES: What do you think *envious* means?

☐ jealous
☐ happy
☐ afraid

5. S-T-R-E-T-C-H: Do you think Lynne thinks Will is brave? Tell why.

Bacon and Egg

Bacon and Egg sat side by side on a breakfast plate. Bacon said he was the better food because he was crispy. Egg said he was better because he was fluffy. Bacon bragged about his long, rectangular shape. Egg boasted about his beautiful round shape. Bacon said people always called him *yummy*. Egg **insisted** that even more people called him *yummy*. "Hey, what does *yummy* mean, anyway?" asked Bacon.

"I'm not sure," said Egg.

Just then a girl sat down at the table and gobbled them both up. "*Yummy, yummy!*" she announced with a smile.

KEY QUESTIONS

1. COMPARE: How are Bacon and Egg similar?

2. CONTRAST: How are they different?

3. TONE: Is the tone of this story silly or serious? How do you know?

4. CONTEXT CLUES: What do you think *insisted* means?

- ☐ strongly suggested
- ☐ disagreed
- ☐ sunny side up

5. S-T-R-E-T-C-H: What's your favorite breakfast food? Imagine and tell what it might say.

Mila and Kylie

Mila and Kylie were best friends. Mila was tall, and Kylie was short. Mila wore glasses, while Kylie did not. Mila's best subject in school was math. Kylie was really good at social studies. Mila enjoyed playing sports. Kylie's favorite **pastime** was reading novels. But they both loved, loved, loved the pop star, Dustin Fleeber.

So when the girls bumped smack dab into Dustin at the local mall, they both had the same reaction: They fainted.

KEY QUESTIONS

1. COMPARE: How are Mila and Kylie similar?

2. CONTRAST: How are they different?

3. INFERENCE: Why do the girls faint when they see Dustin Fleeber?

4. CONTEXT CLUES: What do you think *pastime* means?

- ☐ the future
- ☐ the old days
- ☐ fun activity

5. S-T-R-E-T-C-H: Who is your favorite performer? How would you behave if you saw that person in real life?

LITERARY TEXT: CONFLICT AND RESOLUTION

My Furry Alarm Clock

It used to be really hard to get me up in the morning. When my alarm clock rang, I'd fling my arm across the bed without realizing it and turn off the alarm. Then, unfortunately, I'd go right back to sleeping like a baby. My mom shook me and shouted my name. But getting me to wake up was like pulling teeth. Then I **devised** a plan. Now, every morning my mom opens my door and lets Jules, our puppy, into my room. Jules leaps onto my bed and starts licking my face. There's just no way to sleep through that!

KEY QUESTIONS

1. CONFLICT: What is the narrator's conflict?

2. RESOLUTION: How does he or she resolve the conflict?

3. CONFLICT AND RESOLUTION: Complete this sentence frame: In this story, the conflict is _____, and the resolution is _____.

4. CONTEXT CLUES: What do you think *devised* means?

☐ thought up
☐ shouted
☐ asked

5. S-T-R-E-T-C-H: A simile compares two unlike things using the word *like* or *as*. *Roar like a lion* is a simile. Can you find two in this story? Use each in a new sentence.

LITERARY TEXT: CONFLICT AND RESOLUTION

It Sounds Nice, But . . .

Kiana's aunt Lana lived in Hawaii. One day she emailed Kiana and invited her to come for a visit. "We'll go swimming and snorkeling," Aunt Lana wrote. "It'll be great!" Kiana thought it sounded amazing, but there was just one **obstacle**: She was afraid of water. The idea of swimming in the ocean terrified her. When she was about to tell Aunt Lana she couldn't come, she saw a story on the news about people who took special swimming classes to get over their fear of water. Kiana wrote down the information and gave it to her dad. "Can I sign up for lessons?" she asked.

"Sure thing!" he responded.

KEY QUESTIONS

1. CONFLICT: What is Kiana's conflict?

2. RESOLUTION: How does she resolve the conflict?

3. CONFLICT AND RESOLUTION: Complete this sentence frame: In this story, the conflict is _____, and the resolution is _____.

4. CONTEXT CLUES: What do you think *obstacle* means?

☐ trick
☐ problem
☐ fear

5. S-T-R-E-T-C-H: What do you think happens next in the story?

Hot Sauce Hal

Hal's parents told him to finish dinner or there would be no dessert. On this particular night, that was a big problem. Hal had to find some way to finish his asparagus. He hated asparagus. But he loved hot sauce. So he poured hot sauce on his asparagus. Now it was **palatable**. Hal managed to finish his asparagus, and he was ready for a treat. Dessert turned out to be apple pie. Hal liked apple pie okay, but it sure wasn't his favorite dessert. So guess what he poured on it? Delicious!

KEY QUESTIONS

1. CONFLICT: What is Hal's conflict?

2. RESOLUTION: How does he resolve the conflict?

3. CONFLICT AND RESOLUTION: Complete this sentence frame: In this story, the conflict is _____, and the resolution is _____.

4. CONTEXT CLUES: What do you think *palatable* means?

☐ unpleasant to taste
☐ pleasant to taste
☐ green and red

5. S-T-R-E-T-C-H: Create an advertising jingle for hot sauce narrated by Hal.

Nice Snakey

A woman from the zoo visited Donald's school. One of the animals she brought was a snake. She gave each kid a chance to touch it. "Don't worry," said the lady. "It's tame. It won't bite you."

Even so, Donald was frightened. But he badly wanted to **overcome** his fear. When it was Donald's turn, he closed his eyes and pretended he was petting a kitten. It wasn't as bad as he expected.

"Nice kitty," said Donald.

"What?!" asked the surprised zoo lady.

"I mean, nice snakey."

KEY QUESTIONS

1. CONFLICT: What is Donald's conflict?

2. RESOLUTION: How does he resolve the conflict?

3. CONFLICT AND RESOLUTION: Complete this sentence frame: In this story, the conflict is _____, and the resolution is _____.

4. CONTEXT CLUES: What do you think *overcome* means?

☐ run
☐ improve
☐ slither

5. S-T-R-E-T-C-H: What fear have you overcome? Tell about it.

A Pet, Please!

Jayden really wanted a pet. The trouble was that his apartment building had a strict no-pets rule. He thought that maybe the landlord, Ms. Osaki, would make an exception if Jayden asked really nicely.

"Ms. Osaki, I really want to get a dog. Just a small dog. What do you say?"

"I say, there's a **stringent** no-pet policy in this building."

A few days later Jayden tried again. "How about a cat?" But Ms. Osaki said no. "How about a parrot?" But again, the answer was no.

Finally, Jayden tried one last time. "How about a goldfish?"

"Sure," said Ms. Osaki with a wink. "I have three goldfish myself."

KEY QUESTIONS

1. CONFLICT: What is Jayden's conflict?

2. RESOLUTION: How does he resolve the conflict?

3. CONFLICT AND RESOLUTION: Complete this sentence frame: In this story, the conflict is _____, and the resolution is _____.

4. CONTEXT CLUES: What do you think *stringent* means?

☐ unfair
☐ strict
☐ new

5. S-T-R-E-T-C-H: Why does Ms. Osaki wink at the end of the story?

Roly Poly's Big Day

Roly Poly's friend Snail lived at the top of a pile of dirt. It was a **modest** dirt pile. Nevertheless, it took tiny Roly several hours to climb to the top. When he did, he enjoyed a great afternoon with Snail. *Yeehaw*! In fact, Roly had so much fun that he lost all track of time. The sun was starting to set. Roly had promised his mom he'd be home by dark. *Uh-oh*. How could he climb down that dirt pile on his tiny legs?

Then he had an idea. He rolled himself into a ball. Then— *wheeeeee*! He rolled down the dirt pile and all the way home.

KEY QUESTIONS

1. CONFLICT: What is Roly Poly's conflict?

2. RESOLUTION: How does he resolve the conflict?

3. CONFLICT AND RESOLUTION: Complete this sentence frame: In this story, the conflict is _____, and the resolution is _____.

4. CONTEXT CLUES: What do you think *modest* means?

☐ embarrassed
☐ small
☐ fancy

5. S-T-R-E-T-C-H: *Onomatopoeia* is a word that sounds like its meaning, such as *yippee*. Can you find two examples in this story? Use each in a new sentence.

Bella and the Ravens

The Ravens were Bella's favorite band. So Bella was sad when she found that her concert seats were so far away from the stage. Then things got even worse. People started standing on their seats. Bella stood, but she couldn't see over everyone. Then she had an idea. This was not a movie. She didn't have to see it. Bella sat down, listened, and the music sounded awesome.

"Did you see the Ravens?" everyone at school asked the next day.

"I didn't see them, but I heard them," said Bella. "They were **phenomenal**."

KEY QUESTIONS

1. CONFLICT: What is Bella's conflict?

2. RESOLUTION: How does she resolve the conflict?

3. CONFLICT AND RESOLUTION: Complete this sentence frame: In this story, the conflict is _____, and the resolution is _____.

4. CONTEXT CLUES: What do you think *phenomenal* means?

☐ really loud
☐ really bad
☐ really great

5. S-T-R-E-T-C-H: What is your favorite band? What do you like about them?

All Out of Books

Leo loved reading books. No matter what the subject, Leo would read it. But one day, Leo ran out of books to read. He had read every single book in his town's library. For a book-lover like Leo, this was a serious problem. He went to Mr. Ruiz, the librarian, and told him his **predicament**.

"Do you remember all those books?" asked Mr. Ruiz. "Even the ones you read five years ago?" Leo admitted that he didn't.

"Well, there you go," said Mr. Ruiz. "You can start all over from the beginning!" And that's what Leo did.

KEY QUESTIONS

1. CONFLICT: What is Leo's conflict?

2. RESOLUTION: How does he resolve the conflict?

3. CONFLICT AND RESOLUTION: Complete this sentence frame: In this story, the conflict is _____, and the resolution is _____.

4. CONTEXT CLUES: What do you think *predicament* means?

☐ difficult situation
☐ big secret
☐ odd opinion

5. S-T-R-E-T-C-H: Does Leo think Mr. Ruiz's suggestion is a good one? How do you know?

Purple Penelope

Penelope was an elf. She loved her life, except for one small problem: She hated the color green. And most of what elves wear is green. The other elves **assured** Penelope she would grow to like green. That didn't happen. Instead, she decided to get a different-colored outfit. The other elves said this was a bad idea. Penelope didn't listen. She chose a purple vest, purple shoes, and a purple hat with a purple feather. Guess what? Nothing terrible happened. Instead, the other elves started telling Penelope things like, "What an awesome hat! I think I'll get myself an orange one."

KEY QUESTIONS

1. CONFLICT: What is Penelope's problem?

2. RESOLUTION: How does she resolve the conflict?

3. CONFLICT AND RESOLUTION: Complete this sentence frame: In this story, the conflict is _____, and the resolution is _____..

4. CONTEXT CLUES: What do you think *assured* means?

☐ strongly suggested
☐ begged loudly
☐ argued softly

5. S-T-R-E-T-C-H: What type of elf outfit would you like to wear? Describe it.

Ming's Race Against the Clock

When Ming finished the get-well card she was making for her grandfather, she **glanced** at the clock. *Oh, no!* thought Ming. It was already

ten minutes to five. The post office closed at 5:00. She wanted to get the card in the mail today so her grandfather would get it as soon as possible. She ran to her bike, but the back tire was flat. *Oh, no!* thought Ming. Then she had an idea. She threw on her roller skates, grabbed the card, and flew the three blocks to the post office. She handed the card to the postal worker, just as he was locking the door!

KEY QUESTIONS

1. CONFLICT: What is Ming's conflict?

2. RESOLUTION: How does she resolve the conflict?

3. CONFLICT AND RESOLUTION: Complete this sentence frame: In this story, the conflict is _____, and the resolution is _____.

4. CONTEXT CLUES: What do you think *glanced* means?

☐ broke
☐ wished
☐ looked

5. S-T-R-E-T-C-H: What is your favorite way to get around? Why?

The Adventures of Bob the Rock

When Maddie was in third grade, she read *The Adventures of Bob the Rock*. The **tedious** book was about a boring gray rock named Bob. All Bob did was sit there for 128 long pages. Maddie had a hard time finishing the book because it always put her to sleep. Now, Maddie was in the sixth grade. She had a math test tomorrow, and she just couldn't get to sleep. But Maddie had an idea: She found the old rock book. Then she got into bed and started reading. Very quickly, she dozed off. The next day, she woke up well-rested and ready to take on the world . . . or at least the math test!

KEY QUESTIONS

1. CAUSE: What causes Maddie to get sleepy?

2. EFFECT: What effect does reading the rock book have on Maddie?

3. CAUSE AND EFFECT: Complete this sentence frame: In this story, the cause is _____, and the effect is _____.

4. CONTEXT CLUES: What do you think *tedious* means?

☐ action-packed
☐ funny
☐ boring

5. S-T-R-E-T-C-H: What tricks do you use to help yourself fall asleep? Tell about them.

The Myth of Icarus

Icarus and his father, Daedalus, were imprisoned in a maze with no way out. But Daedalus was a talented craftsman. He built two pairs of wings from feathers and wax. He and Icarus strapped on the wings and began to fly. At last they were free! Daedalus warned Icarus not to fly near the sun. "If you do," he said, "the wax will melt, the wings will fall apart, and you'll fall into the sea." But Icarus didn't **heed** his father's warning. He was so excited to be flying! He went higher and higher. But just as his father warned, the wax on his wings started to melt, and Icarus plummeted into the sea.

KEY QUESTIONS

1. CAUSE: What causes Icarus to fall into the sea?

2. EFFECT: What effect does flying high have on Icarus and his wings?

3. CAUSE AND EFFECT: Complete this sentence frame: In this story, the cause is _____, and the effect is _____.

4. CONTEXT CLUES: What do you think *heed* means?

☐ pay attention to
☐ ignore
☐ forget

5. S-T-R-E-T-C-H: Do you think building the wings was a good idea or bad idea? Tell why.

Too Many Cookies

Pete loved chocolate chip cookies more than anything. His mom told him that sweet treats were best eaten **sparingly**. Just one or two, every now and then. But when it came to chocolate chip cookies, Pete thought the more the better. One Saturday, after his mom baked a big batch of delicious chocolate chippers, Pete couldn't help himself. He had two. Then he had two more. And then three more! What Pete ended up with then was a giant stomachache!

KEY QUESTIONS

1. CAUSE: What causes Pete to have a stomachache?

2. EFFECT: What effect does eating the cookies have on Pete?

3. CAUSE AND EFFECT: Complete this sentence frame: In this story, the cause is _____, and the effect is _____.

4. CONTEXT CLUES: What do you think *sparingly* means?

☐ often
☐ not often
☐ quickly

5. S-T-R-E-T-C-H: What lesson do you think Pete learns from this experience?

A Hamster Trick

Jayla had the best desk in class. She sat right near Harvey's cage. Harvey was her class's pet hamster. One day, Jayla tapped her pencil on her desk three times. Harvey stood up on his **hind** legs. Interesting. Jayla tried tapping her pencil once. Nothing. She tapped twice. Nothing. But when she tapped three times, Harvey stood up again. "I taught Harvey a trick!" exclaimed Jayla.

She tapped her pencil three times. Sure enough, Harvey stood up. Everyone clapped, including her teacher. *Hmmmm*, thought Jayla. I wonder if four pencil taps will cause Harvey to do a different trick?

KEY QUESTIONS

1. CAUSE: What causes Harvey to stand up on his hind legs?

2. EFFECT: What effect does three pencil taps have on Harvey?

3. CAUSE AND EFFECT: Complete this sentence frame: In this story, the cause is _____, and the effect is _____.

4. CONTEXT CLUES: What do you think *hind* means?

☐ strong ☐ rodent ☐ back

5. S-T-R-E-T-C-H: What trick do you imagine four pencil taps might cause Harvey to do? Tell about it.

The Class Plant

Jack took the class plant home over the summer. He promised his teacher that he would take good care of it. He would put it in a sunny spot in his yard and water it **diligently**. "It will be bigger and greener than ever," Jack told Ms. Kinsella. But then Jack's summer got really busy. He went to soccer camp for a week. Then his cousin came to visit for ten days. During that time, Jack forgot all about watering the plant. When he finally remembered and went to check on it, the little plant was brown and nearly dead.

KEY QUESTIONS

1. CAUSE: What causes the plant to nearly die?

2. EFFECT: What effect does Jack's forgetfulness have on the plant?

3. CAUSE AND EFFECT: Complete this sentence frame: In this story, the cause is _____, and the effect is _____.

4. CONTEXT CLUES: What do you think *diligently* means?

☐ nervously
☐ infrequently
☐ carefully

5. S-T-R-E-T-C-H: How do you think Jack feels at the end of the story?

Snow at Last!

Shelby had been waiting and waiting for snow. Finally, one night in early December, it came. She woke up to find a blanket of snow on the ground. Shelby rushed outside to build a snowman. She had just finished it, when her dad **insisted** that it was time to leave for school. All day, Shelby couldn't wait to get home to see her snowy new friend. But at the end of the day when she walked outside, the sun was shining and the air was warm. Almost all of the snow had melted. When she got home—*Oh, no!* The snowman was just a puddle.

KEY QUESTIONS

1. CAUSE: What causes the snowman to melt?

2. EFFECT: What effect does the warmer weather have on the snowman?

3. CAUSE AND EFFECT: Complete this sentence frame: In this story, the cause is _____, and the effect is _____.

4. CONTEXT CLUES: What do you think *insisted* means?

☐ remembered
☐ demanded
☐ rushed

5. S-T-R-E-T-C-H: What would you say to cheer Shelby up?

The Teeth-Flossing Superhero

When Archie went to the dentist he had a cavity. Again! He told Dr. Smithers that he always brushed his teeth but didn't floss them. Dr. Smithers looked displeased. She said Archie had to become a teeth-flossing *superhero*! She gave him a big roll of floss and sent him on his way. Archie was determined to be the best teeth flosser ever, so he began flossing morning, noon, and night. He flossed when he read books and when he watched TV, too. Six months later, his **perseverance** had paid off. "No cavities!" Dr. Smithers said with a bright, white smile.

KEY QUESTIONS

1. CAUSE: What eventually causes Archie to have no cavities?

2. EFFECT: What effect does flossing have on Archie's teeth?

3. CAUSE AND EFFECT: Complete this sentence frame: In this story, the cause is _____, and the effect is _____.

4. CONTEXT CLUE: What do you think *perseverance* means?

☐ continued hard work
☐ tooth-brushing
☐ dentist appointment

5. S-T-R-E-T-C-H: Why is Dr. Smithers displeased at the beginning of the story? How does she feel at the end?

The Cantankerous Giggles

Every time Shawna heard the word *cantankerous*, she would giggle. One time she was watching a movie and a character said, "cantankerous." She giggled. Another time she was reading a novel and came across the word. She giggled. It was just such a silly sounding word, thought Shawna.

One day, Shawna woke up in a cranky mood. Her friends asked what was wrong. They told her to cheer up. They tried everything, but nothing worked. Then her friend said, "You seem very **cantankerous** today."

Shawna started to giggle. She felt better already.

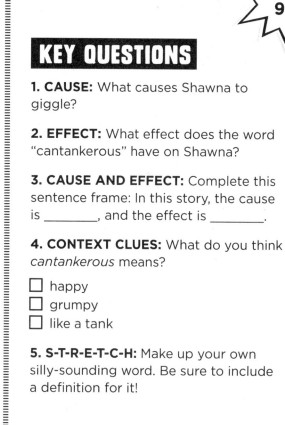

KEY QUESTIONS

1. CAUSE: What causes Shawna to giggle?

2. EFFECT: What effect does the word "cantankerous" have on Shawna?

3. CAUSE AND EFFECT: Complete this sentence frame: In this story, the cause is _____, and the effect is _____.

4. CONTEXT CLUES: What do you think *cantankerous* means?

☐ happy
☐ grumpy
☐ like a tank

5. S-T-R-E-T-C-H: Make up your own silly-sounding word. Be sure to include a definition for it!

Annie Steps Up

"Step right up," said the **barker** at the county fair. "Knock down a stack of milk bottles with a ball. Win a prize."

Annie was a talented softball pitcher. So she paid a dollar for three throws. She missed them all. She tried again, and it happened again. What was wrong? Annie realized she was throwing overhand. She paid for another turn. This time she threw underhand, the way she did when she played softball. With her very first toss, Annie knocked down the bottles. She kept knocking them over until she won big stuffed bears for each of her friends.

KEY QUESTIONS

1. CAUSE: What causes Annie to knock down the bottles?

2. EFFECT: What effect does throwing underhand have on the bottles?

3. CAUSE AND EFFECT: Complete this sentence frame: In this story, the cause is _____, and the effect is _____.

4. CONTEXT CLUES: What do you think *barker* means?

☐ a very loud dog
☐ a person who attracts customers
☐ a person who sells cotton candy

5. S-T-R-E-T-C-H: Is Annie a generous person? How do you know?

Chain Reaction

Arjun's science project was incredible! First, she rolled a blueberry down a ramp. The blueberry bumped into a grape. That caused the grape to roll down another ramp. A cup of milk sat at the edge of a table. When the grape bumped it, the cup fell and spilled milk on the floor. A cat walked up and started to lap the milk. A dog on a leash spotted the cat. It **lunged** at the cat. The leash was attached to a light switch. Off went the light. "Bravo!" said Arjun's teacher. "I'm going to use this little pencil to give you a big 100."

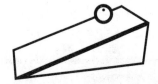

KEY QUESTIONS

1. CAUSE: What is the first thing that happens in the experiment?

2. EFFECT: What is the last thing that happens in the experiment?

3. CAUSE AND EFFECT: Complete this sentence frame: In this story, the (first) cause is _____, and the (last) effect is _____.

4. CONTEXT CLUES: What do you think *lunged* means?

☐ moved forward suddenly
☐ danced slowly
☐ tiptoed backwards

5. S-T-R-E-T-C-H: Use your imagination to describe a chain of events in which a tiny action leads to a huge event.

SAMPLE ANSWERS

PREDICTION

What's Going On? (Card 1)
1. I think Maddie will open the door and get a surprise party.
2. No, I think Maddie will consider it a great day because she has a party.
3. Maddie's mom wants her to think she forgot Maddie's birthday.
4. *Jubilant* means "thrilled."
5. Answers will vary.

Opposite Robot (Card 2)
1. The opposite robot cleans up the lab.
2. She would tell the robot to stay awake.
3. The text says, "The robot broke into a silly dance."
4. *Command* means "order."
5. Answers will vary.

Homework Headache (Card 3)
1. I think both Mario and Derrick will get in trouble.
2. No, I think they will both get in trouble because the teacher told both of them to stay after school.
3. Derrick doesn't always do his homework and sometimes he cheats.
4. *Conscientious* means "hardworking."
5. Mario let Derrick copy his homework because he wanted to be a good friend. It was not wise because they will both get in trouble.

Planet Wingding (Card 4)
1. I think the cow flies.
2. The narrator might see a pig and horse with wings.
3. Earth and Wingding both have people and animals, but on Wingding every creature can fly.
4. *Bizarre* means "very strange."
5. Answers will vary.

Flying High (Card 5)
1. I think Meg will swing on the trapeze.
2. I think she will feel excited and proud that she faced her fear.
3. She feels afraid.
4. *Vanquish* means "beat."
5. Answers will vary.

Baking Cookies (Card 6)
1. I think the cookies will burn.
2. I think she will tell Natalie that she was supposed to watch the cookies.
3. The story says, "The TV was so loud, she didn't hear the timer when it beeped."
4. *Dollops* are "blobs."
5. Two examples of onomatopoeia are *growled* and *beeped*. (Sentences will vary.)

Sharing Sherice (Card 7)
1. Sherice will take Lisa on a one-ticket ride.
2. Lisa might say, "I sure love gum!"
3. Sherice is generous. She thinks about others.
4. *Adored* means "loved."
5. Answers will vary.

A Day at the Beach (Card 8)

1. Yes, I think he will get burned.
2. The story says that he burns when he's in the sun too long and he forgot to put on sunscreen.
3. The story says, "His favorite activity, though, was building a gigantic sand castle."
4. *Slather* means "spread thickly."
5. It's a good idea to put on sunscreen when you're in the sun.

Lucy's Odd Luck (Card 9)

1. Something amazingly good happened to Lucy.
2. I think Lucy's luck will be normal on Saturday because it will no longer be Friday the 13th.
3. Her grandmother bakes her seven cookies.
4. *Harbinger* means "sign."
5. She's supposed to have bad luck on Friday the 13th, so good luck is odd.

Six Scoops (Card 10)

1. The Frisbee hits Mark's ice cream cone and knocks it out of his hand.
2. Mark catches the Frisbee and licks the ice cream at the same time.
3. His cone has chocolate, vanilla, strawberry, peach, mint, and rainbow.
4. *Precarious* means "likely to fall."
5. Answers will vary.

INFERENCE

Where's Dinner? (Card 11)

1. I think Zeke ate the meat.
2. She says that because she thinks Zeke ate the meat.
3. Kyle and his mother will look for Zeke to see if he ate the hamburger meat.
4. *Exuberantly* means "excitedly."
5. Answers will vary.

The Favor (Card 12)

1. Zoe lends Luke her cell phone. Luke takes pictures for Zoe at the zoo.
2. The pictures show the animals at the zoo, so she knows what she would have seen if she'd been there.
3. Luke is a good friend because he does a nice thing for Zoe.
4. *Dispirited* means "sad."
5. Answers will vary.

Up a Tree (Card 13)

1. Juan wants to be the best at tree-climbing.
2. Juan is stuck, and they need a ladder to get him down.
3. They are cousins.
4. *Like the back of my hand* means "very well."
5. Answers will vary.

The Big Night (Card 14)

1. Ava is practicing her lines because she's in a play.
2. Ava has been in performances before. The author says that she always has jitters before she goes on stage.
3. This is set backstage before a play begins.

4. *Jitters* means "nervous feelings."

5. *Knock 'em dead* means "do a great job." Sentences will vary.

Ty's Jeans (Card 15)

1. Now that the weather is cool, it's time for long pants.

2. Ty has grown taller over the summer.

3. Ty lives in Texas.

4. *Peculiar* means "strange."

5. Answers will vary.

Mystery of the Muddy Footprints (Card 16)

1. The duck tracked in the mud.

2. The duck has only two feet and they're webbed.

3. This story is silly, because the animals behave like people.

4. *Drenched* means "very wet."

5. Answers will vary.

The Birthday Breakfast (Card 17)

1. She says they're the best because she loves that Dan made them for her.

2. She probably can, but she doesn't care.

3. She is 38.

4. *Summoned* means "called."

5. Answers will vary.

Fly Away Home (Card 18)

1. The story is about a ladybug.

2. The ladybug has a scarlet shell with black dots.

3. The ladybug is the narrator.

4. *Scarlet* means "red."

5. *Snug as a bug in a rug* means "very comfortable." Sentences will vary.

Cherry Lemonade (Card 19)

1. The day was hot and sunny.

2. The cherry ice pops melted.

3. The text says, "Soon there was a long line at his stand."

4. *Inspiration* means "sudden brilliant idea."

5. Answers will vary.

Go Fly a Kite (Card 20)

1. It takes place in fall. Sania puts on a sweater, and she jumps on freshly raked leaves.

2. The kite won't stay up because it isn't windy.

3. The story says, "Instead she decided to jump in a freshly raked pile of leaves.

4. *Hurtling* means moving "quickly and wildly."

5. Answers will vary.

CHARACTER

A New Home (Card 21)

1. Tam cares about plants and likes to rescue things.

2. Tam thinks plants shouldn't be thrown out. Mrs. Simon thinks it's okay to throw out plants.

3. The plant is not healthy. The story says it was crooked and yellowish, with just a few little leaves.

4. The saying *a green thumb* means "good with plants."

5. I think the plant might become healthier, because Tam and her mom will care for it.

The Late Leaf (Card 22)

1. The leaf is stubborn and worried. It doesn't like change.
2. The other leaves have fallen already.
3. An alliteration in the story is: "flip, float, and fly."
4. *Budge* means "move."
5. Answers will vary.

To Go or Not to Go? (Card 23)

1. Max is shy and gets nervous.
2. Meeting new people makes Max nervous.
3. That is the title because Max has to decide whether or not to go to the party.
4. *Warm up* means "get comfortable."
5. I think Max will go because he remembers that he usually has fun at parties after he warms up.

A Girl Called N.V. (Card 24)

1. N.V. is a jealous and envious person.
2. N.V. sounds the same as the word that fits her character—envy.
3. N.V. would want a skateboard.
4. *Envy* means "jealousy."
5. Answers will vary, but should describe someone who is full of energy.

No Bones for You (Card 25)

1. Toby is selfish, inconsiderate, and boastful.
2. Baxter probably feels hurt that Toby won't share.
3. The author says, "Whenever Toby the sheepdog got a new bone, he buried it in the backyard."
4. *Crowed* means "bragged."
5. Answers will vary.

Waiting for the Bus (Card 26)

1. Olivia is thoughtful and kind.
2. Olivia feels sorry for the old woman because it is hard for her to get around.
3. It is winter. It is cold, and it started to snow.
4. *Frail* means "weak."
5. Answers will vary.

José's Favorite Subject (Card 27)

1. José brags a lot and thinks he is great.
2. His favorite subject to talk about is himself.
3. Anita walks away because she gets tired of José's bragging.
4. *A piece of cake* means "easy."
5. Answers will vary.

Zany Zelda (Card 28)

1. Zelda is wacky. She does what she wants to do.
2. Zelda is very zany.
3. Answers will vary, but should involve something zany.
4. *Donned* means "put on."
5. Answers will vary.

Donnie at the Dentist (Card 29)

1. Donnie is a dreamer. He has a big imagination.
2. He uses his imagination to escape.
3. He's happy that he's done at the dentist.
4. *Dread* means "fear."
5. Answers will vary.

Marvin Starts His Day (Card 30)

1. Marvin is careless and really messy.
2. Another good title is *Messy Marvin*. (Other answers possible.)
3. Marvin had cornflakes, orange juice, and bacon.
4. *Draped* means "arranged loosely."
5. Answers will vary.

SETTING

Big Score, Small Prize (Card 31)

1. The story takes place at an arcade.
2. It takes place in current times because it has games and flashing lights.
3. An example of personification is, "The machine spit out a long row of tickets."
4. *Ambled* means "walked."
5. Omar got the high score, but the prizes were little things like a comb and an eraser.

After Hours (Card 32)

1. The story takes place in a museum.
2. It takes place in the evening. The title is *After Hours*, and it says all the visitors had gone home.
3. The text says, "A portrait called *Prince Gregory* put on giant sunglasses."
4. *Somber* means "serious."
5. Answers will vary.

Seeing the Sights (Card 33)

1. The story takes place in Washington, D.C.
2. It is spring. The clue of the cherry blossoms helped me figure this out.
3. She sees the White House, the Capitol, the National Gallery of Art, the Lincoln Memorial, and the cherry blossoms.
4. *Majestic* means "grand."
5. Answers will vary.

Did You Hear That? (Card 34)

1. The story takes place in the boys' backyard.
2. It is nighttime.
3. Cal is nervous and fearful.
4. *Nudged* means "poked."
5. "Snoring like a buzz saw" and "out like a light" are similes.

Time for Broccoli (Card 35)

1. The story takes place in a grocery store.
2. It takes place in the day. The text said, "the sun was shining through the front window."
3. She chooses broccoli instead of carrots.
4. *Summoned* means "called upon."
5. Answers will vary.

The Lion's Roar (Card 36)

1. The story takes place at the zoo.
2. It's a sunny day. The text said it was "a bright summer day."
3. "For the ten thousandth time" is a hyperbole.
4. *Slinking* means "moving quietly."
5. Owen wants to leave because the lion's roar scares him.

The Trip Home (Card 37)

1. The story takes place on an airplane.
2. It is nighttime. The sky is dark and Ryan has just had dinner.
3. Ryan lives in Boston. The story says, "He was now on his way back home to Boston."
4. *Descent* means "movement downward."
5. Ryan feels proud because his mom is the pilot.

A Perfect Sand Castle (Card 38)

1. It takes place on the beach.
2. It's summer. School is over, and it is 85 degrees.
3. The waves washed the sand castle away.
4. *Admire* means "view with pleasure."
5. I think the sand castle will wash away. I would tell the boys to build one farther from the water. (Advice will vary.)

What a Catch! (Card 39)

1. The story takes place at a baseball game.
2. It is night. I know because it says they are under bright lights.
3. She loves her granddad. I can tell because she beams at him.
4. *Devoured* means "eaten quickly."
5. Two onomatopoeias in this story are "whizzing" and "crack."

Floating Toothpaste (Card 40)

1. The story takes place in outer space.
2. The narrator can see the whole planet Earth.
3. Both. The narrator has to do work, but does flips and has fun.

4. *Vital* means "important."
5. Answers will vary.

POINT OF VIEW

Three Birthdays in One (Card 41)

1. The reader can see into Lia's, Tia's and Pia's minds.
2. The story is told in third-person omniscient.
3. The text says, "He tried to bounce the ball off his head—and *CRACK*!"
4. *Loathed* means "hated."
5. Answers will vary.

Humpty Dumpty: The Truth (Card 42)

1. The narrator is Father Goose.
2. The point of view is first person.
3. He was bouncing a soccer ball off his head.
4. *Perspective* means "point of view."
5. Answers will vary.

The Magic Show (Card 43)

1. The narrator's name is Melvin Gelby.
2. The story is told in first person.
3. The number he has ready is 10,654,982,773.
4. *Bellowed* means "shouted."
5. Answers will vary.

Allie Gets Her Own Room (Card 44)

1. The reader can see into Allie's mind.
2. The story is told in third-person limited.
3. Allie is relieved because she won't have to fight Iris for the bigger room.
4. *Domineering* means "bossy."
5. Answers will vary.

Trader Tom (Card 45)

1. I think his name is Tom because the story's title is *Trader Tom*.
2. This point of view is first person.
3. He trades the comic book for an action figure.
4. *Absurd* means "silly."
5. Answers will vary.

Banana Peel Boy to the Rescue (Card 46)

1. No, you can't tell anyone's point of view.
2. The point of view is third-person limited.
3. The resolution is that Cheetah Man slips on Banana Peel Boy. Then he goes to jail.
4. *Villain* means "bad guy."
5. Answers will vary.

Ugh! Braces! (Card 47)

1. The reader can see into Suki's mind, her mom's mind, and Ben's mind.
2. The story is told in third-person omniscient.
3. She thinks getting braces is going to make her life miserable.
4. *Making a mountain out of a molehill* means "exaggerating."
5. Answers will vary.

The Sixth-Grade Champ (Card 48)

1. The narrator's name is Linda Breen.
2. The story is told in first person.
3. I know Linda won because she spelled the word that Jamal missed.
4. *Slew words like dragons* means "spelled words well."
5. Answers will vary.

Just Chillin' (Card 49)

1. I would guess this character is always busy and never relaxes.
2. The point of view is first person.
3. The second slush was lime.
4. *Intense* means "very powerful."
5. Answers will vary.

Puffed-up Pete (Card 50)

1. Yes, you can tell what Pete is thinking. He is thinking that he is amazing. Yes, the other fish are thinking that Pete thinks he's great.
2. This story is told in third-person omniscient.
3. Pete gets so proud that he puffs up.
4. *Deflate* means "let air out."
5. Answers will vary.

TONE

Not-So-Blue Monday (Card 51)

1. The main tone is cranky.
2. The story changes to happy at the end because the narrator gets an *A* on a test.
3. Because this Monday wasn't entirely bad. It had a happy ending.
4. *Detest* means "hate."
5. Answers will vary.

I'm the Best! (Card 52)

1. The tone is boastful.
2. The narrator doesn't seem likeable because he thinks he's better than everybody else.
3. He probably doesn't have friends because he always brags.
4. *Intimidate* means "make nervous."
5. Answers will vary.

Missing Scooter (Card 53)

1. The tone is sad.
2. The narrator feels sad that Scooter is moving.
3. The narrator is a dog
4. *Mournfully* means "sadly."
5. Answers will vary.

At the Snail Races (Card 54)

1. The tone is silly.
2. Sally is very excited. (Answers will vary.)
3. Snail #2 has a white shell.
4. *Determination* means "strong-willed."
5. Answers will vary.

The Shadowy Figure (Card 55)

1. The tone is spooky.
2. It takes place in a dark, old house on a lonely hill, which seems scary.
3. Two examples of onomatopoeia are "creak" and "screeeeech."
4. *Scrumptious* means "delicious."
5. Answers will vary.

Fast Friends (Card 56)

1. The tone is lonely.
2. The tone is happier. Kim has made some friends.
3. The phrase, "the most friendless girl in the whole universe" is a hyperbole.
4. *Extraordinarily* means "especially."
5. Answers will vary.

The Worst Day Ever (Card 57)

1. The tone is embarrassed.
2. This is probably not the worst day. Mike is overreacting because he was embarrassed.
3. Two examples of onomatopoeia are "Aagh!" and "Splat!"
4. *Mortified* means "embarrassed."
5. Answers will vary.

Babysitting (Card 58)

1. The tone of the story is sarcastic.
2. No, the narrator means the opposite.
3. She gets food on her face because she's just a baby.
4. *Nuisance* means "pest."
5. Answers will vary.

Tortoise Time (Card 59)

1. The tone of this story is nervous.
2. This story is exaggerated because the tortoise is afraid of simple things.
3. The text says, "Tortoise heard humans walking in the woods."
4. *Retracted* means "pull in."
5. Answers will vary.

My Baby Brother (Card 60)

1. The tone is humorous.
2. She's mad at him, but she also loves him.
3. "They" refers to her parents.
4. *Cherished* means "adored."
5. Answers will vary.

Extreme Burger (Card 61)

1. The theme is: Fancy isn't always better.
2. Theo learns that sometimes simple is best.
3. "When the Extreme Burger arrived, it was as big as a spaceship," is a hyperbole.
4. *Ghastly* means "horrible."
5. Answers will vary.

The Myth of King Midas (Card 62)

1. The theme is: Being greedy can get you in trouble.
2. Being rich is not the most important thing.
3. The king is very greedy.
4. *Restored* means "returned."
5. It's a curse because it ends up ruining his life.

A Change of Plans (Card 63)

1. The theme is: When you go back on your word, people won't trust you.
2. You should do what you say you're going to do.
3. Jen is irresponsible.
4. *Irked* means "annoyed."
5. Answers will vary.

Zack's Sax (Card 64)

1. The theme is: Practice makes perfect.
2. I learned that to get better at something takes practice.
3. Two similes are "like an old hound dog howling at the moon" and "like a car screeching to a halt."
4. *Halt* means "stop."
5. Answers will vary.

The Ants and the Grasshopper (Card 65)

1. The theme is: Work hard and be prepared.
2. He learns that it's important to plan ahead.
3. According to the text, "the grasshopper just wanted to sing and play and enjoy himself."
4. *Serenaded* means "sang to."
5. Answers will vary.

All You Can Chew (Card 66)

1. The theme is: You can have too much of a good thing.
2. Clara learns not to overdo things, like chewing too much gum at once.
3. Three examples of onomatopoeia are "Chomp, chomp!" "Pop!" and "Snap!"
4. *Resolved* means "strongly decided."
5. Answers will vary.

The Boy Who Cried Wolf: An Aesop's Fable (Card 67)

1. The theme is: When you lie a lot, people won't believe you when you tell the truth.
2. The boy learns it's not a good idea to trick people.
3. He is bored. The text says, "He wanted something interesting to happen."
4. *Jeopardy* means "danger."
5. "Cry wolf" means to claim there's a problem when there's really not. It is a bad thing to do because people won't believe you after that.

Best Friends (Card 68)

1. The theme is: Always be loyal to your true friends.
2. Heidi learns that it's important to treat your friends well.
3. Heidi's new friend's name is Tina.
4. *Inseparable* means "always together."
5. It means that she had a good friendship, and she lost it.

A Little Surprise (Card 69)

1. The theme is: Great gifts can come in small packages.
2. Manny learns to not judge something by its size.
3. The numbers were: 38-1-21.
4. *Massive* means "huge."
5. Answers will vary.

The Acrobat and the Apples (Card 70)

1. The theme is: Sometimes it's a good idea to ask for help.
2. Larry learns that he can get what he wants with the help of others.
3. The text says, "Larry was the ringmaster of the circus."
4. *Fancied* means "thought."
5. Answers will vary.

COMPARE AND CONTRAST

The Great Brownie Bake-off (Card 71)

1. Both brownies are sweet and chocolatey.
2. Beth's brownies are small and gooey. Dan's are big and cakey.
3. He eats 100.
4. *Controversy* means "disagreement."
5. The story is not realistic. The names aren't realistic. The whole town would not eat just brownies. And the mayor couldn't eat 100 brownies.

No Place Like Home (Card 72)

1. They both love where they live and wouldn't want to trade places.
2. Mina likes the city. Padma likes the suburbs.
3. She sees skyscrapers and yellow taxi cabs.
4. *Suburbs* means "areas outside the city."
5. Answers will vary.

Scaredy Monsters (Card 73)

1. Todd and Gwen both love teddy bears and sunny beaches. They hate dark caves, and they are both scaredy monsters.
2. Todd likes cupcakes and birds chirping. Gwen likes rice pudding and opera singing.
3. Todd and Gwen hate dark caves because caves are scary.
4. *Preferred* means "liked better."
5. Answers will vary.

Strongman Versus Ant (Card 74)

1. They are both strong.
2. The strongman is big. The ant is tiny.
3. The text says, "The strongman lifted a 500-pound weight."
4. *Impressed* means "respectful."
5. Answers will vary.

Postcards From Camp (Card 75)

1. Both love their camp. Both are learning a lot.
2. Their activities are different. Aisha never wants to leave, but Ella is ready to go home.
3. Aisha calls her *Lu,* and Ella calls her *Lucy-Goosey*.
4. *Elated* means "very happy."
5. Answers will vary.

What Pet Should We Get? (Card 76)

1. Both dogs and cats need to be fed every day and given attention.
2. Dogs need to go for walks, and they get lonely when they're left alone. Cats are less social, and don't mind being on their own.
3. I think they will get a pet cat.
4. *Social* means "likes to be around others."
5. Answers will vary.

Pen Pals (Card 77)

1. Both Puffin and Penguin are birds who eat fish. They both love palm trees.
2. Puffin is little, can fly, and lives at the North Pole. Penguin is big, can waddle, and lives at the South Pole.
3. An example of alliteration is "pen pals picked the perfect place."
4. *Journey* means "trip."
5. Answers will vary.

Who's Scared? (Card 78)

1. Will and Lynne both have fears.
2. Will is afraid of roller coasters, and Lynne is afraid of snakes.
3. Lynne screams because she's scared of snakes.
4. *Envious* means "jealous."
5. Answers will vary.

Bacon and Egg (Card 79)

1. Bacon and Egg are both foods that people say are yummy.
2. Bacon is crispy, long, and rectangular. Egg is round and fluffy.
3. Bacon and Egg can talk, so it's a silly story.
4. *Insisted* means "strongly suggested."
5. Answers will vary.

Mila and Kylie (Card 80)

1. They are both girls who love Dustin Fleeber.
2. Mila is tall with glasses. She is good at math and likes to play sports. Kylie is short with no glasses. She is good at social studies and likes to read novels.
3. They fainted because they were both excited to see Dustin Fleeber.
4. *Pastime* means "fun activity."
5. Answers will vary.

CONFLICT AND RESOLUTION

My Furry Alarm Clock (Card 81)

1. The narrator can't get out of bed in the morning.
2. Her puppy wakes her up.
3. In this story, the conflict is that the narrator can't get out of bed in the morning, and the resolution is that her puppy wakes her up.
4. *Devised* means "thought up."
5. Two similes are "sleeping like a baby" and "like pulling teeth." (Sentences will vary.)

It Sounds Nice, But . . . (Card 82)

1. Kiana is afraid of water.
2. She decides to sign up for lessons to get over her fear.
3. In this story, the conflict is that Kiana is afraid of water, and the resolution is that she signs up for lessons to get over her fear.
4. *Obstacle* means "problem."
5. I think Kiana takes the lessons and goes to Hawaii. (Answers will vary.)

Hot Sauce Hal (Card 83)

1. Hal hates asparagus.
2. He pours hot sauce on his asparagus.
3. In this story, the conflict is that Hal hates asparagus, and the resolution is that he pours hot sauce on it.
4. *Palatable* means "pleasant to taste."
5. Answers will vary.

Nice Snakey (Card 84)

1. Donald is afraid to pet the snake.
2. Donald pretends the snake is a kitten.
3. In this story, the conflict is that Donald is afraid to pet the snake, and the resolution is that he pretends the snake is a kitten.
4. *Overcome* means "improve."
5. Answers will vary.

A Pet, Please! (Card 85)

1. Jayden wants a pet, but his building doesn't allow pets.
2. He decides to get a goldfish, which is allowed.
3. In this story, the conflict is that Jayden wants a pet but the building doesn't allow pets, and the resolution is that he decides to get a goldfish, which is allowed.
4. *Stringent* means "strict."
5. She winks because she's going to let him get a goldfish despite the rule because even she has goldfish.

Roly Poly's Big Day (Card 86)

1. Roly has to get home by dark, and it is late.
2. Roly rolls down the dirt pile and all the way home.
3. In this story, the conflict is that Roly has to get home fast, and the resolution is that he rolls all the way home.
4. *Modest* means "small."
5. Two examples of onomatopoeia are "*Yeehaw*" and "*wheeee*." (Sentences will vary.)

Bella and the Ravens (Card 87)

1. Bella can't see the band at the concert.
2. Bella decides to just listen and not worry that she can't see.

3. In this story, the conflict is that Bella can't see the band, and the resolution is that she just listens to the music.
4. *Phenomenal* means "really great."
5. Answers will vary.

All Out of Books (Card 88)

1. Leo has run out of books to read.
2. Leo decides to reread all the books in the library.
3. In this story, the conflict is that Leo has run out of books to read, and the resolution is that he decides to reread all the books in the library.
4. *Predicament* means "difficult situation."
5. Leo must think Mr. Ruiz's suggestion is good, because he follows his advice.

Purple Penelope (Card 89)

1. Penelope doesn't like to wear the color green.
2. She decides to wear the color purple.
3. In this story, the conflict is that Penelope doesn't like to wear green, and the resolution is that she wears purple instead.
4. *Assured* means "strongly suggested."
5. Answers will vary.

Ming's Race Against the Clock (Card 90)

1. Ming needs to get to the post office before it closes.
2. Ming uses roller skates to get there fast.
3. In this story, the conflict is that Ming needs to get to the post office before it closes, and the resolution is that she uses roller skates to get there fast.
4. *Glanced* means "looked."
5. Answers will vary.

CAUSE AND EFFECT

The Adventures of Bob the Rock (Card 91)

1. Reading *The Adventures of Bob the Rock* makes Maddie sleepy.
2. It makes her fall asleep.
3. In this story, the cause is reading *The Adventures of Bob the Rock,* and the effect is that it makes Maddie fall asleep.
4. *Tedious* means "boring."
5. Answers will vary.

The Myth of Icarus (Card 92)

1. Icarus flies too close to the sun.
2. It causes the wax to melt, and his wings fall apart.
3. In this story, the cause is flying too close to the sun, and the effect is that the wings melt and fall apart.
4. *Heed* means "pay attention to."
5. Answers will vary.

Too Many Cookies (Card 93)

1. Pete eats too many cookies.
2. Eating too many cookies leads to Pete's having a stomachache.
3. In this story, the cause is eating too many cookies, and the effect is a stomachache.
4. *Sparingly* means "not often."
5. I think Pete learns that eating too many sweets is not a good idea. (Answers will vary.)

A Hamster Trick (Card 94)

1. Jayla taps her pencil three times.
2. Harvey stands on his hind legs.
3. In this story, the cause is Jayla tapping her pencil three times, and the effect is that Harvey stands on his hind legs.
4. *Hind* means "back."
5. Answer will vary.

The Class Plant (Card 95)

1. Jack forgets to water it.
2. The plant nearly dies.
3. In this story, the cause is forgetting to water the plant, and the effect is that the plant nearly dies.
4. *Diligently* means "carefully."
5. I think Jack probably feels sad that he hasn't taken care of the plant.

Snow at Last! (Card 96)

1. The sun comes out and the weather turns warmer.
2. It causes the snowman to melt.
3. In this story, the cause is warmer weather, and the effect is that the snowman melts.
4. *Insisted* means "demanded."
5. Answers will vary.

The Teeth-Flossing Superhero (Card 97)

1. Archie flosses morning, noon, and night.
2. He has no cavities six months later.
3. In this story, the cause is flossing morning, noon, and night, and the effect is no cavities.
4. *Perseverance* means "continued hard work."
5. Dr. Smithers is displeased at the beginning because Archie doesn't floss. She's happy at the end because he's become a good flosser and has no cavities.

The Cantankerous Giggles (Card 98)

1. Shawna giggles when she hears the word "cantankerous."
2. The word makes her giggle.
3. In this story, the cause is hearing the word "cantankerous," and the effect is that it makes Shawna giggle.
4. *Cantankerous* means grumpy.
5. Answers will vary.

Annie Steps Up (Card 99)

1. Throwing underhand causes Annie to knock down the bottles.
2. Annie knocks them down.
3. In this story, the cause is Annie's switching to throwing underhand, and the effect is that she knocks downs the bottles.
4. *Barker* means a "person who attracts customers."
5. Yes. Annie gave the stuffed bears she won to her friends.

Chain Reaction (Card 100)

1. A blueberry rolls down a ramp.
2. The light turns off.
3. In this story, the cause is a blueberry rolling down a ramp, and the effect is that a light turns off.
4. *Lunged* means "moved forward suddenly."
5. Answers will vary.